Equipoise: Insights Into Foundational Astral Training

The Franz Bardon Community

Equipoise: Insights Into Foundational Astral Training

The Franz Bardon Community

Falcon Books Publishing Ltd
2019

2019 First Edition Published by
FALCON BOOKS PUBLISHING
www.falconbookspublishing.com

Copyright © 2019 Falcon Books Publishing All rights reserved.
No portion of this book, except for brief review, may be reproduced, stored in a retrieval system, or transmitted in any form or by any means—electronic, mechanical, photocopying, recording, or otherwise—without the written permission of the publisher.
For information contact:
sales@falconbookspublishing.com
71-75 Shelton Street
Covent Garden
WC2H 9JQ
London

Image credits
Cover art by Tanya Robinson
Franz Bardon photo within the public domain.

All efforts have been made to identify and correctly attribute photographic credits. Should any error have occurred, it is entirely unintentional.

Edited by Julian Rees

First Printing: 2019

ISBN 13: 978-986-97705-2-1

Dedication

The co-authors and editors of this book would like to dedicate it to the Best Friends Animal Society. Thank you for your efforts to advocate kindness toward animals.

TABLE OF CONTENTS

Dedication..iii
Table of Contents...vii
Foreword..x
PART I: INTROSPECTION..1
   1. The Soul's Garden – Guido Cesano...3
   2. Introspection – A Path to Develop Self-Awareness – Sapnali Chetia..9
   3. Creating The Soul Mirrors – Ewen..29
   4. Balancing The Humors – A Traditional Approach to the Work of The Soul Mirrors –Martin Faulks..35
   5. Mirror of The Soul – Angel of God..42
   6. A Favorite Activity of Saturn – William R. Mistele.......................45
   7. Soul Mirror Exercises – Ilyas Rahhali...47
   8. The Second Level of Introspection – Ray del Sole.......................51
   9. The Unveiling of Introspection – Tamoken...................................53
   10. With Great Power Comes Great Responsibility – Gregory Jeremiah Touw Ngie Tjouw...58
   11. Soul Mirrors/Introspection/Triggers – Steve Vadney....................62
   12. Goal Setting and Introspection – Aaron Wolfe............................67
PARTt II: UNDERSTANDING MAGICAL EQUILIBRIUM..................71
   1. The Multidimensional Equilibrium Process - Muhammad Husain Ali Baig...73
   2. The Magical Balance – Angel of God..76
   3. The Four Pillars of the Temple – Crystalf Maibach.......................79
   4. On Magical Equilibrium – William R. Mistele..............................86

5. E.Q.U.I.P.O.I.S.E. – Angelica de los Santos..................99
6. The Need for a Balanced Development – Ray del Sole..................100
7. Some Aspects of Magical Equilibrium – Ray del Sole..................101
8. Let's Have Dinner – Eric Summers..................103
9. What is Magic Equilibrium? –Richard A. Wright..................104

PART III: ESTABLISHING MAGICAL EQUILIBRIUM..................111
1. Active Imagination Technique: Dear Subconscious, Let's Be Friends? – J.L. Amato..................112
2. The Magic of Water – Angel of God..................124
3. To See Each Life Opportunity as a Lecture and a Possibility to Transform your Trait – Johannes Kul..................127
4. Divine Purpose: Finding Your Why for Achieving Magical Equilibrium, Adepthood, and Beyond - Mahabija..................132
5. How to Deal with Emotional Resistance – Gabriel Moreira..........138
6. Establishing Magical Equilibrium – A Miscellany of Information – Christian Lindo Ntanzi..................140
7. The Six-Pronged Attack – Ilyas Rahhali..................144
8. How do I Control my Subconscious Mind? -Tanya Robinson.......148
9. Why You Should Work with The Four Elements – Ray del Sole...161
10. Training with The Four Elements – Ray del Sole..................163
11. A Qabbalistic Approach for the Magical Equilibrium – Ray del Sole..................165
12. The Emerald Tablet – Ronda Starkey..................167
13. How Greed Obstructs Efficient Self-Transformation – Virgil......175
14. Conscious Eating and the Tetragrammaton – Virgil..................178

Foreword

In his book Initiation into Hermetics, Franz Bardon makes it very clear that the student of magic must establish a state of magical equilibrium within himself before he can safely work with the potent energies of the four elements. This work of establishing magical equilibrium is challenging because it requires the student to make major changes in his personality by rooting out deeply-ingrained negative traits and bad habits, as well as by establishing positive traits and virtues that may previously have been foreign to the student's identity. Given the magnitude of this endeavor to transform oneself, it is not surprising that many people find this task very intimidating.

The thing is, within the Bardon community, there is a wealth of knowledge related to self-transformation; after all, many people have been through the first two steps of IIH. Unfortunately, this knowledge is pretty much all in peoples' heads. Since most beginning students of the Bardon system can't read minds, they don't have access to this knowledge. The problem lies in getting the knowledge from peoples' heads into a medium that everyone can access and learn from. This book is designed to help solve that problem. Over the course of the first few months of 2019, Tanya and I reached out to numerous individuals we knew to be serious students of the Bardon system and asked them to share whatever helpful knowledge and insights they had regarding the astral work of Steps 1 and 2. In response, many were generous enough to spend the time and effort to write the essays, stories, and poems compiled in this book. The total number of contributors to this book numbers more than two dozen - over twice as many as the number I expected to have when I first envisioned this book back in April. These pieces of writing capture the important things they learned from their experience successfully establishing magical equilibrium, and I am immensely grateful to them for sharing their knowledge.

Virgil
October, 2019

Figure 1: Franz Bardon

Part I: Introspection

1. The Soul's Garden – Guido Cesano

Our Soul is like a big garden.

It can be a beautiful garden, a true paradise – in fact the word paradise comes from the greek 'paràdeisos' meaning garden – or it can be a terrible hell.
Not all gardens are the same. The difference is made by the gardener.

In some gardens grow beautiful plants, flowers of all colors, fruit trees, there are paths, water games and these small paradises are populated with all kinds of beings – fairies, goblins, animals. In the air you can feel delicate aromas and the chirping of birds is a real delight.
The gardener is always cheerful, whistles and works hard to make his garden the best possible.
He removes weeds, protects the most delicate flowers, controls plant growth so that it does not become invasive and keeps everything in harmony and balance. His garden is beautiful and it is a pleasure to stay there. He never gets tired because the energy of his garden is really high.

Other gardens are a disaster, weeds everywhere, plants that grow irregularly, ponds clogged with putrid water, dry leaves, dead twigs … here live few animals, mostly mosquitoes, rats and other annoying beings.
The gardener sleeps, he is lazy, often drunk. He has no incentive to make his garden more beautiful. He has no interest. He has no enthusiasm and has completely lost his passion. Being in his garden is a really bad experience.
The energy's vibration is very low and the gardener is always tired, lazier and lazier, always ready to complain. He continually curses the bad conditions to which he is subjected. He blames God, destiny, external events, but never looks at himself.

Still **other gardens are very simple**. A green lawn, low cut, without frills, without too many weeds, without flowers.

Very simple to maintain, sufficiently ordered, without major problems. But poor. The energy in this type of garden is not as low as in the previous one, but it is weak. There is little enthusiasm, little passion.

The gardener does the minimum possible, thinking that one day, who knows when, he will be well disposed to create a better garden, much more interesting ... but he already knows that there will be a lot of work to do ... too much work ... it will be tiring ... but it will ... yes it will ... but not now ... now it keeps things simple. Few weeds, but also few flowers, few plants ...

In the Soul's Garden, flowers, bushes, fruit trees and all the furnishings are representations of the most beautiful virtues, good habits, good thoughts, good deeds.

All weeds and harmful animals are vices, bad habits, bad thoughts and bad behaviors.

In the system of Hermetic Initiation by Franz Bardon we have a Black Mirror that represents all the negative aspects of our Soul and a White Mirror that represents all the positive aspects.

A mistake that is often made and that I made in the approach to the Mirrors of the Soul is to give almost all the attention to the Black Mirror and very little to the White Mirror. This was my big mistake.

I focused on removing the weeds from my Soul Garden so I got used to identifying negative things.

I started with all my faults, my shortcomings in all the roles of my life, from personal aspects, to work, to family and social relations to health.

Then, I continued with introspection asking myself 'What are the factors that prevent me from achieving my goals?'

So for each of my unreached goals there are different impediments, different aspects that hinder my path. They can be beliefs, wrong thoughts, ingrained emotions, incorrect or missing actions.

Identifying all the weeds in the garden, I kept looking and practiced seeing the glass half empty, even when it was half full.

But there is another aspect.

PART I: INTROSPECTION

Focusing only on the things to be eliminated, on the negative things, after a while it becomes boring, frustrating and de-motivating. Because weeds are always popping up. As soon as you finish cleaning a flowerbed ... tac !! Here you find another small weed that is being born.

As a good gardener, I was not at all satisfied with my work. In fact I was very frustrated, because despite all the work I did, my garden was no longer beautiful. It was simply mediocre.

So I started to understand what I was missing. The Balance between the Mirrors was missing, much more than the Balance between the Elements.

The work of the Mirrors is done both with the Black Mirror and with the White Mirror – the half-empty glass and the half-full glass.

It is done with what we want to eliminate, what we want to take away from ...

And it is done with what we want to achieve, what we want to go to ...

The stick ... and the carrot.

The White Mirror represents my best features ... but not only this.

It also represents what I want to become. In the White Mirror there are also all the virtues that I want to cultivate, but which are still very little or only potential. I can have a virtue in one field, but not in another.

I can be courageous in some circumstances, but not in others. So, I have the seed of courage, but I need to expand it more.

Perhaps they are only thoughts, ideas, or I have these things only occasionally ... but I have them and I have every intention of manifesting them.

Looking at the positive is much more motivating.

Wouldn't my garden be more beautiful with beautiful plants, colorful flowers, water features, statues, fruit trees, singing birds, fishes in the pond? Wouldn't it be nicer than a mediocre all-green turf?

Looking at the positive in us puts us in a positive mood.

And our attitude, our mental and emotional state, heavily influences the way we live our life, our adventures and also practice the exercises and also our results.

Why does someone spend years and years on the first exercises on the first level, while others take a few weeks?

What is the driving force that some have and many others do not?

Why do some people excel in sport or business in a short time, while others struggle so much to produce few results?

Why do some people recover quickly and others never recover despite all the practices they can do?

The key is attitude. The key that sets the process in motion is given by positive emotions and the way we relate to life.

For some, life is a hard and tiring battle; for others a beautiful and exciting game.

What we do is important. But how we do it is even more so.

From some techniques we can achieve no result, we can get worse, especially if we begin subconsciously to cultivate frustration, nervousness and a sense of continuous failure … or we can achieve full success very quickly.

What makes the difference is the state of our Soul's Garden.

Practicing magical breathing with enthusiasm is something quite different from practicing it mechanically.

Practicing the cold shower with a sense of adventure and challenge is something quite different from practicing it mechanically.

For example, if I want to increase enthusiasm, I can use all the techniques suggested by Bardon such as magical breathing, magical eating, auto-suggestion.

But here a problem is triggered. We cannot absorb enthusiasm rationally. It is not a mental pill that I put in a glass of water and by drinking it I automatically become more enthusiastic. Something is missing … it doesn't work that way.

My rationality has been my big limit for a long time. I asked myself several times if it was a question of faith – f I had to believe it to make the technique work. And it really didn't work.

It was not enough to think that by drinking a glass 'loaded' with a rational concept of enthusiasm one can acquire that characteristic. Does not work.

PART I: INTROSPECTION

And so I thought and reread the instructions well and thought again. And I had a flash of insight.

'I have to imagine absorbing enthusiasm. Imagine. Don't believe.

So it is not a question of faith, but of imagination.'

Thus it becomes child's play. Children play with imagination constantly. No problem if they believe something or not. They play, they imagine making meatballs with sand and having fun. And they really have fun. They don't have to believe that it is true to have fun.

I must not believe that the glass of water has become 'enthusiasm'. I have to imagine drinking a magic potion that makes me more enthusiastic and feel it, fake it also, like a game.

The cold and dry imagination has no impact on the subconscious ... and so the old model returns always into play.

I need to know what enthusiasm means.

I must have a clear picture of what enthusiasm is. A feeling. So I can watch videos of enthusiastic people ... for example Jim Carrey in the movie 'Yes Man' and internalize physiology, sensations, words, tone of voice ...

When I have a clear image I can transform it into sensation ... feel it ... recreate it and amplify it every time.

And by enhancing the flower of Enthusiasm in the garden of the Soul, spaces for other weeds such as laziness, boredom, procrastination ... are greatly reduced

It is not easy to compile the White Mirror with all our virtues, our strengths, our positive habits.

We are conditioned to see the negative side of things, or we are conditioned to be modest.

Yet we all have positive qualities.

Some qualities are very evident and are our strengths, those that allow us to excel in some areas of our life.

Others may be less obvious but are still embryonic, sporadic, infrequent ... but they are there. And we can develop them, make them grow.

We can also take models of successful people, in whatever sector we are interested in and begin to identify which traits we want to develop.

> Do we want to become better at achieving our goals? Increase the charisma, enthusiasm, leadership? What are the characteristics of the Fire Element that I want in my Soul?

Do we want to become smarter? More creative? More able to communicate? What are the characteristics of the Air Element that I want to solidify within me?

Do we want to become better at relationships? More empathetic? More altruistic? More loving? Who has these characteristics of the Water Element?

Do we want to become more productive? More organized? More methodical in our work? What are the characteristics of Earth that I want to amplify?

The thoughts we have in our mind naturally tend to manifest themselves, with more or less time depending on the attention we give them, their frequency and energy. They determine our state of mind, which in turn influences the decisions we make in life and consequently our actions, our behaviors and our results.

Therefore it is important to create the Black Mirror of our Weak Points, just as it is important to create the White Mirror of our Strong Points, even if they are still potential and still have to grow, to operate in a coordinated way and to further enhance the Virtues opposed to the Vices.

It is a mistake to give more importance to the Black Mirror than to the White Mirror. This is a work of Balance and Harmony.

The Black Mirror tells us from what we have to go away.

The White Mirror shows us the luminous direction we have to go, or the Inner Harmony. And it is here that it is important to seek to develop a good Balance between the Elements, because defects must all be eradicated or weakened to the maximum.

In the Soul's Garden, day by day, we starve the weeds removing water and nourishment, while we increasingly devote our energy and our attention to the beautiful and colorful flowers of the Virtues.

PART I: INTROSPECTION

2. Introspection – A Path to Develop Self-Awareness – Sapnali Chetia

Ask the path, learn the way, but listen to your heart, and ride the wave.

Introspection is an exercise to realize your true self, to become conscious and aware of your true self, to feel, to understand and to accept your true self without any self-manipulation.

It helps you to understand your inner nature, and makes you aware of the role your feelings and your emotions play in your life. It includes understanding and appreciating the strengths as well as the weaknesses in your personal character.

A normal person usually sleeps at night, goes through some dreams, wakes up and goes on to live his day. One day follows the other as the same emotional patterns, patterns of behavior and problems repeat themselves. Then a day comes when the problems have become too large to ignore, but by that point usually it is simply too late to wake up. The damage has already been done, and the only thing left is to learn a lesson for the future and to move on the best one can.

Introspection allows one to avoid such situations and weed out problems before they become too large to solve. It is about being proactive and learning the lessons of life without going through unnecessary suffering in order to learn them. It is about getting things right the first time.

It also allows one to consciously recognize one's strengths and weaknesses, the positive and negative aspects of one's soul.

The 'soul mirror' is a spiritual mirror that reflects your true self. It helps you to gain insights into your hidden abilities and flaws. The main purpose of the soul mirror is to give you an idea of the hidden positive and negative aspects of your personality.

The negative aspects are responsible for negative thinking, negative emotions and negative patterns of behavior. Positive aspects are the aspects within us which have the potential to make us feel loved, to empower us, to encourage us but often these become overshadowed by the effects of the negative aspects in our lives

Let's take an example. You look at a child and you feel love towards the child. You want to hug the child and play with her – a positive aspect of your personality – then suddenly a worrying thought crosses your mind 'Oh no! I have to work on that project, tomorrow's the deadline, I don't have any time for this.' The negative has overshadowed the positive.

Another example – let's say you have a very serious attitude towards spiritual progress. You look at the child when she is playing, laughing, having fun. You look at her and say to yourself 'No, I don't have time for this, I have to work on my spiritual journey, I have to train.' This attitude is also a blockage and is blocking the positive aspects of your personality. It lacks balance.

Once you understand what is blocking you, what the behavior patterns are that are blocking you from experiencing full abundance, freedom and joy in all aspects of your life, and what their root causes are, you will make real progress by getting rid of your negative aspects and working on enhancing the positive aspects in your personality.

At times we may feel that we do not have control over our own actions. Sometimes we do not understand why we feel the way we feel. Our emotions – fear, distress, worry, anger and so on, may seem to come out spontaneously without having much control or even having awareness of them. People follow the same emotional patterns for so long that these start to feel completely normal and in many cases they are completely unaware that these patterns even exist.

It is very common to see people who, for example, get angry all the time but find their behavior to be completely normal – 'So what if I get angry? It is normal to get a little bit angry'. Sometimes they may not be aware of the anger at all and may even get more angry when confronted about it – 'Me, angry? Never! I am one of the politest people and get angry only when there is no option. I don't want to talk to you anymore'.

This is certainly not limited to anger but extends to all negative emotions such as those of fear, worry, jealousy and so on. What is important is to be completely aware of such emotions and patterns that we exhibit in our life. This includes those aspects which have been with us for a very long

PART I: INTROSPECTION

time and feel completely normal to us. Being aware of our negative aspects with complete truthfulness is the first step towards attaining personal freedom.

This is an important step for any spiritual aspirant. Many people choose to ignore this step as it might not seem very important in the beginning but if a student is serious about walking on the path of light, he must learn to see through himself. A student must see himself, feel himself, understand himself and then accept himself.

I have seen many people who don't want to work on this step because when they sit down they get bored easily, or get tired; some are in a rush, some manage always to find out seemingly genuine excuses to avoid this step. But the root cause of this behavior is that they are running from themselves subconsciously. Introspection involves facing oneself. People avoid their shadow self subconsciously because facing the shadow will bring out deeply buried pains, memories and past incidents on to the surface of consciousness which can be an unpleasant and uncomfortable experience, which is why they just do not want to confront these issues, feel them, and understand them. It is hard for them to accept the truth.

Their subconscious mind finds an escape route in the form of excuses, excuses that perfectly align with their ego.

An example – take a person who has had a bad childhood. He was misunderstood, bullied, ignored and rejected by his mother, by his friends in his school and by women in his adulthood.

He has a deep wound buried in his heart. The wound is made from a lack of love, respect and acceptance. The rejection he faces will slowly generate anger, the negative side of the fire element but the source is lack of love which belongs to the water element. During his adulthood he will be rebellious, not respectful, not loving, and not caring about his mother. There are many paths that fate could present him with.

1. He could resort to escapism with alcohol or become a drug-addict to escape his reality – a lack of earth element.

2. To find love and acceptance, he will create emotions of lust, the negative form of water element, and have sex with any

woman to feel loved and accepted in his core, but without success.

3. He could find a woman who genuinely loves him, but in this case he can become desperate, possessive, suspicious. His past would make him fear losing the person, because she would have become too precious for him and such desperation can become a prison for the woman.

4. In a rare case he will make the choice to come to the magical and the spiritual world, and then fate would unfold another set of paths in front of him. He would have the option to choose the path of light or the path of illusions. In many cases people in such situations are driven by anger or frustration. So in his spiritual journey, real progress would come only when he understands and accepts the root cause of his shadow patterns. This individual is destined to learn. He might learn through chaos or he might learn by his own choice. This transformation will be the first step and it will occur whether he likes it or not. Resistance to any changes from this transformation will only make things more chaotic for him because this transformation will force him to face the wounds and reality from which he has been running for so long. The purpose of this transformation is to heal the negative memories, which may hinder his spiritual progress if left unhealed, with love and acceptance – the water element.

5. Not all the paths have to be negative – he might learn to generate the love in his heart which he never received from others in his life and decide to spread love. Many higher souls have to face troubles in their childhood but it is seen as an opportunity from a higher perspective.
If you are able to deal with the situation that is going on inside you then you get an ability to deal with it and heal the situation outside. You will be able to experience great life-changing transformations and that will only bring you closer to your spiritual missions.

PART I: INTROSPECTION

Introspection and de-programming

Our mind is constantly conditioned, starting from the moment we are born in the material world. A benefit of carrying out introspection on yourself is that you can de-program your mind and see your life and your circumstances as they really are, and with an entirely new perspective.

For instance, society often conditions people to believe that being spiritual is somehow associated with being 'generous poor', and that they should never take money for their services and so on. Imagine that you are a person who believes that taking money for any spiritual service is wrong, or a person who believes that they do not need money because they are spiritual. As a result of a bias like this it could become extremely difficult for such people to earn money in the physical realm.

Another case could be of a person who imagines that he is not worthy of money. This feeling of not deserving money can create a major blockage in the path towards personal freedom and happiness.

In all these scenarios you can easily sense the programmed mind filled with half-knowledge, society-induced biases and self-doubts.

Through introspection you will understand the higher perspective of having money and abundance in your life. You will understand that money is needed to live on this earth; it provides freedom, happiness, security and support to your spiritual mission. And you will see through these biases which society tries to present to all of us.

When you have money, you have the freedom to work on your spiritual path without any obstacles, and this freedom will provide you with happiness. At the same time you will have security and be able to support your spiritual personal goals and your spiritual mission on this earth.

Such self-imposed restrictions don't just exist around the topic of money, but also around love, success, abundance and so on. A person can be made to believe they can never be successful because no one in their family has ever been successful, or that they can never find true love because their parents could not find true love. Such biases can be completely unconscious and yet cause great blockages to the individual.

These beliefs can sometimes become so deeply ingrained in the subconscious that they may be very difficult to identify and work on.

However it is vital to see through these via deep introspection in order to gain true freedom.

Understanding the hidden negative aspects of our personality

Introspection, when carried out properly, can reveal hidden negative aspects of our personality, of which we may not be conscious. The human ego can be very skilled at self-manipulation and at hiding such traits. To make matters worse, it can be very easy to be offended if someone points out such traits in us, since that is seen as an attack on our ego and invokes our defensive nature. Hence, it is up to us to maintain a very high standard when working on introspection, and to be ruthlessly truthful when looking into ourselves.

I once told a person that he needed to work on his anger. This comment provoked him, and he looked down on me and got back at me, saying that this anger was a part of his intense nature, implying that there was nothing wrong with the anger and even trying to attribute it as a positive aspect of his personality.

Let's take a moment to examine what happened. This person had a problem with anger. But when I pointed this out, he felt offended, and even violated. His only option then was to get back at me and defend himself in any way possible. And that meant justifying his negative attribute as a positive one.

The ego needs a lot of love and feels attacked in such situations. But in such a case this defence is an act of self-manipulation. Unfortunately, it is very easy to believe in such lies that we make to ourselves, and to be unaware of our negative traits. It is therefore very important to be truthful and to de-condition yourself from such dispositions when working on introspection.

Another example – a person was behaving with me in a very negative, arrogant and dictatorial way, and justified her behavior by saying that she carried out introspection on herself regularly and hence she obviously could not be in the wrong. This is just another form of self-deception. Her work on introspection had not managed to go beyond the layers of her ego and her negative aspects were unconsciously controlling her. She was not aware of

PART I: INTROSPECTION

the negatively dominating aspects of her personality. This unawareness is a major spiritual trap, and a belief that a superficial level of introspection is enough can create many obstacles on the spiritual path.

One more example would be spiritual groups where everyone is trying to please their master, giving rise to the consequent emotions of jealousy and competition that arise amongst peers. This is a problem that is very widespread and yet lacks awareness and is not much acknowledged.

These emotions are often very insidious and can easily sidetrack one's progress on the path. Look at yourself the way a master would look at you, acknowledging all your positive as well as negative traits for what they are. Remember that introspection is a very personal exercise. There is no one judging you, and hence no need to defend yourself. It is an exercise that everyone has to do at the beginning of their spiritual training – no exceptions. No spiritual master will ever look down at you for your negative traits; they only ask that you become aware and conscious of them, and work on them. So do not let your ego get in the way of spiritual progress, and identify and work on all your imbalances.

Guilt and forgiveness

Self-hatred is often the first step on the path to darkness. We have all made mistakes in our past. Probably no one has been incarnated on earth who has not made mistakes. While it is important to have high standards for our behavior, it is also equally important to forgive ourselves for any mistakes we have made in the past and work on healing and repairing the damage they might have caused.

Introspection can often make us aware of mistakes we might have made in the past and of which we may not so far have been aware. We might have caused harm to others knowingly or unknowingly. It is important to analyze these and make efforts to heal them, but it makes no sense to dwell on them. Guilt is a luxury that a spiritual seeker simply cannot afford. There is a need to forgive ourselves as well as to ask for forgiveness from any other parties involved.

Introspection is not a magic wand that would rid us of our past karma. But it can ease our situation by making us aware of the mistakes we may have made in the past and by showing us a path to heal these, so that we can learn our lessons and move on. It helps us to avoid making the mistake again.

A soul mirror meditation

When I started working on my soul mirror, I followed a method that I was guided towards by my intuition. I will try to share that method in this section.

The method involves focusing on some of the strong and emotionally charged memories from the past, and examining their relation with the present. I personally started by focusing on my life and memories from my life – my childhood years, my teenage, followed by my present life. I made a list of every strong memory that I could recollect from these parts of my life. This process became at times very hard and painful for me because some of the painful memories made me feel as if I was living them over and again.

Try this exercise. Sit in your meditative position and breathe deeply. Feel that every breath brings a sense of calmness to your body. Inhale and exhale deeply and softly. Stay in this state for a while and then take your intention towards any recent incident that had made you feel upset.

Rewind the incident in your mind and try to see the situation from a higher perspective. Imagine that you are not you anymore, but instead you have become a third person observing the incident. Be honest with yourself. Do not manipulate yourself, do not hide anything, and do not become influenced. Contemplate carefully and understand how you behaved in this situation. If someone makes you angry or upset when you think about this incident, then try to forgive that person. Observe your own reaction to the incident. Could your reaction have been any different? What result would that have had on the situation? Observe and think about this with an open mind.

During the entirety of this process you have to be very calm and stable. If you feel agitated then resume slow and deep breathing. Inhale, fill your lungs completely, and then exhale and empty your lungs completely. Do this till you feel comfortable and then resume the process from where you left it.

As you proceed with this exercise, you may recall situations where negative parts of your personality or weaknesses in your personality have

PART I: INTROSPECTION

manifested themselves. Perhaps it's a situation where you needlessly became angry, or perhaps you did not stand up for yourself where you now feel you should have, or maybe you became frightened when there was nothing to be afraid of.

These patterns of behavior are very important to note, and the deeper you go into your meditation, the more incidents and patterns you will recall. Your aim should be to get to the root cause that led to the development of such behavior. As you proceed with the meditation you will realise that these patterns of behavior are like chains that have entangled you all these years and drained you of your energies little by little.

As you continue to remember past situations and circumstances, studying these recollections will take you deeper. You will see how the same negative patterns of behavior have repeated themselves time after time throughout your life. This way you will gain insight on the progression and evolution of these traits through different phases of your life. And contemplating this could lead you to the root cause of the patterns. Such realizations can truly be life-transforming.

After this meditation I usually note down all my discoveries, traits, feelings and sensations that I have observed in my note book.

I am going to take an example of a person called Monty. Let's say you are this person, Monty, and you recently had a fight with your wife. The fight was over not spending enough time with your family. The fight got worse because this time you raised your hand to her, and the result now is that you are headed for a divorce. You are depressed because deep down you know that you are a loving person who would never do anything like that, and yet it is shocking for you that the situation has turned out this way. You want to tell her how much you love her and how much you wished to express that, but you never did.

Instead of giving in, Monty decides to work on himself. He sits in his meditation position and revisits the incident in his mind's eye, trying to see it from a higher perspective. Here he sees himself fighting with his wife and finds it so hard not to blame her for everything. He feels a wave of depression that hits his core, and overwhelming emotions overcome him. It is emotionally difficult and painful to revisit this incident in his mind.

To calm himself down he practices the breathing exercise – breathing deeply.

Slowly, he realigns himself so as to see the incident as a third person observing what happened and he goes over the incident again. He sees the fight as it progresses, how he projected his frustrations of failure upon his wife, and how he yelled at her. Thoughts justifying his behavior and defending his position enter his mind but he rests firmly on his perspective as an outside observer and sees through this behavior. One thought follows the other as a stream of memories from the past flash by in his consciousness.

He can now feel how his words have been draining his wife for so long. After all this was not first time he had behaved with her in that way. And every time he did this, she would feel drained, depressed, hopeless and helpless. She tried to bear with this behavior in the beginning, but soon the fights began. The fights were a warning, one of the many signs that fate had shown him, but he continued blindly without any self-awareness till the situation reached a breaking point. It is a sad realization, but a powerful and awakening one.

He takes a deep breath and goes in deeper into his introspection process, trying to gain a better understanding of his situation and asking God for insights into his behaviour.

Memories from work come back to him. His first job – how he was yelled at and insulted by his boss in front of his colleagues. The anger he felt then was not very different from the anger he now feels toward his wife. He always felt that rush of intense anger at his boss but never expressed it. The anger had been lying there all along, unexpressed and bottled up, waiting to unleash itself. He had felt helpless, hopeless, and miserable as he would hear the whispers and laughs from his colleagues. The pain would hit his heart deeply, making him feel very uneasy.

This anger is due to the feelings of helplessness and frustration that he would feel when his boss would insult him. Their constant accumulation without any outlet for their expression resulted in the creation of a powerful force in his being that was charged with negative energies full of hatred and frustration.

When he reached home, he would unconsciously do the same thing that his boss did to him. He would yell at his wife in an attempt to release his

PART I: INTROSPECTION

frustrations and anger on her. He felt powerful and strong as he could dominate his wife. But he made his wife feel helpless and hopeless.

Then he went deeper into his meditation, and he saw more places where he had felt the same rush of anger. Being insulted by his teachers in school, being unappreciated by his father, his father leaving him and his mother, seeing the weakness in his mother's eyes, all these things made him feel helpless, weak and abandoned. A child who is lost in chaos, who wants to cry and scream but cannot because it will make him seem weak. All these emotions have been continuously stored in his being without being expressed. But they did not go away, and ended up becoming a shadow in his being of which he was unaware.

These realizations made him feel what he had been making himself and his loved ones go through. He noticed how trapped he had become in the repetitive loop of this negative pattern, and how much it was affecting him and his life.

After this realization, he became more conscious about this behavior – 'a rush of anger'. Now that he is fully aware of the pattern, Monty's next work in the coming days would be to figure out possible ways to express these emotions in a way that no one would get hurt, and the anger inside of him could be released.

This is an example of a life-changing transformation that could happen through introspection.

So you can see that a deeper aspect of introspection is to make us aware of our unconscious behavior patterns. Once we learn about them, we can achieve control over them.

For me introspection is like a spiritual broom that sweeps the clutter from our mind and lays down the base of our spiritual foundations. It gives us clarity and this clarity gives us the confidence to make progress in our lives.

After this exercise you should take your diary and make notes on your observations.

In this example, Monty goes through his meditation experience and takes down the following positive and negative traits in his diary

Negative traits

Some of the main traits – in the order of strength of their presence is in the personality: the ones at the top are stronger than the ones at the bottom.

Water element:

1. Helplessness
2. Lack of love
3. Lack of acceptance
4. Feeling offended easily
5. Escapism
6. Lack of understanding
7. Domineering nature
8. Emotional instability
9. Confusion
10. Passiveness
11. Apathy
12. Feeling weak within

Fire element:

1. Jealousy
2. Anger
3. Hatefulness
4. Envious nature
5. Anxiety
13. Abusiveness
14. Frustration
15. Domineering nature
16. Irritation

PART I: INTROSPECTION

Air element:

6. Scornful nature
7. Being prejudiced
8. One-sided nature
9. Insulting nature
10. Lack of commitment
11. Lack of vision
12. Aimlessness
13. Impulsiveness
14. Selfishness
15. Narrow-minded nature

Earth Element:

1. Easily offended
2. Lack of conscience
3. Gloominess
4. Ignorance
5. Melancholy
6. Rigidity
7. Coldness
8. Not being reliable
9. Suspiciousness
10. Unfriendliness

The note-taking process is something very personal and so it is important to take them down in your own, unique way. As far as the categorization of the personality traits into the four elements goes, you have to try your best but at the same time not to worry too much about getting it perfect the first time. As you grow and have more experiences with the elements in your spiritual practice, you will find yourself in a better state to understand and work with them.

At times the same quality can be represented by multiple elements depending on the specific nature of that quality in the person. For example, a person feels that they lack focus in their life – 'lack of focus'. In this case the lack of focus probably means a lack of will-power – fire element. More will-power would bring more focus. But it can also indicate an air and earth element imbalance. Too little of earth and too much of air can cause restlessness and an inability to stick to one thing when working. So you have to look at the elements involved from a personal perspective, and note down what you personally feel regarding the trait involved.

From the summary of traits for Monty, we can see that the root cause here in Monty's case is feeling helpless or weak. The main element he needs is the positive water element. The elements that need balance are fire, air and earth elements.

Know that every person has both positive and negative aspects. For the above story I took only a small fragment of Monty's life.

We have learnt that introspection is all about beginning to know oneself. You will continue to receive more insights on every aspect of your personality by further contemplation.

A method of developing positive personality traits and new abilities

Often we feel that we lack certain personality attributes that we would like to develop. For example, you may lack fire element attributes such as will-power or self-confidence, or an earth element such as persistence, the ability to keep secrets and so on. In general there are specific methods for each ability; for example to increase your will-power, you might focus on your forehead at the point between your eyebrows for a few minutes every day. You may also make an affirmation: 'I have a strong will'. And at a later stage you can also breathe in the fire element directly to realize the ability of a high will-power.

In this section I would like to focus on a general technique to realize virtues in your personality. To continue with the previous example, let's say you are not satisfied with the amount of will-power you possess in your daily life – you find yourself procrastinating a lot, and you are not able to be productive at your work because of lack of focus and will. Hence you have decided to develop a high amount of will-power. With this aim in your mind, you follow the following meditation: imagine a future in which you trained really hard and as a result have reached a high level of self-mastery. Take a look at yourself in this reality. In particular, take note of the kind of will-power you possess in this world. How does it feel to have the will-power of a genuine master? Try to feel this within yourself. Spend some time in this new world where you have truly mastered your will. Feel the potential you have developed.

The truth is that this version of yourself with this highly developed will- power already exists on a higher plane, and is waiting for you to work towards it, to manifest it and bring it into reality. It does not matter if you have a very low amount of will-power right now; the future is wide open. By doing this meditation you can connect with this image that exists in the higher plane and open up the possibility of bringing this image into your life.

Quite often we limit ourselves by our own self-image and biases that exist in our mind. We think of life as a one-dimensional stream of events when in fact we are surrounded by incredible opportunities. This technique will open up those gates of opportunities that would allow you to get in touch with your true potential. It can truly open up new possibilities for your future. It can help you to break through limiting biases within yourself.

This is a general method that applies to all positive personality traits and not just will-power. It can be the first step in realizing personality attributes that you might be weak in.

Inheritance of Personality Traits

People are often deeply connected with their parents. This connection can be very strong and plays an important role in an individual's life. But it is often ignored, and not many are consciously aware of it.

When we are born, we inherit the genes of our parents, and this makes us look somewhat similar to them, and in general, inherit physical attributes from them. As we grow up, we also tend to inherit their emotions, certain behavior patterns and so on from them. These patterns can often be deeply ingrained within our personality and therefore very hard to notice.

As children, when our parents go through tough circumstances in life, we tend to receive and share a portion of their sadness, pain and hurt through them. This happens naturally as children are sensitive to such situations. As we grow up, however, these 'stresses' from the past can become parts of our personality. We might feel emotions of fear, anguish, anger and so on that we feel are parts of our personality, when in truth they could be coming from our parents or close family members. Realizing this then is the first part towards freedom from these imbalances.

The inheritance is not limited to negative attributes but we also receive gifts from our parents in this way, such as intelligence, the ability to handle various situations and so on.

In conclusion, it is important to understand which aspects of our personality we inherit from our parents and our family members so that we can better understand ourselves. It is not an easy task, as we have been living with these attributes for so long that they seem to blend in perfectly with our own personalities, but it is important to discern them so that we can be free and more in touch with our true nature.

Some mistakes

There are some common mistakes that people often make when it comes to introspection and the soul mirror, and I will share some from my own experience.

A limited perspective:

We must not limit our perspective by our thoughts and personal judgments, but instead we should orient our perspective towards the universal truths.

Lack of Open mindedness:

In the beginning, I noticed that when I started working on my soul mirror, I was a bit hesitant and skeptical of the exercise. I was hardly able to find two traits within me because of my rigid nature. I was looking at myself on the surface instead of looking deeper within myself.

The human nature can become very complex due to the constant manipulation from society and because of how complex our behaviors tend to become when interacting with others. This complexity can become a barrier and make our real, inner personality opaque to our perception. To understand and unravel this complex form of our personality, we must learn to have an open mind and compassion towards ourselves. It is only when you dare to open your mind that you would be able to understand the complex nature of the human personality in an easy way.

Unconscious manipulation:

When making my soul mirror, one main mistake that I made was unconscious manipulation. I was manipulating myself during the soul mirror exercise the entire time without knowing it. With many subtle negative traits, instead of going deeper and finding the cause, I would try to find an excuse to justify that negative trait. It is a form of self-deception. This can often be very subtle.

For example, consider this trait – I would feel very offended when someone insulted me. It would be very disturbing for me. I would think that this was not a negative trait because obviously I wasn't at fault for this behavior; the person who insulted me rudely was. However, this is nothing but a subtle form of self-manipulation or ignorance. It is an air element trait – I would become offended too easily by the words of others. I needed to build a tough skin so that others did not hurt me with their words so easily.

Misunderstandings with introspection

When I made progress with the introspection exercise, I noticed that I was being very hard on myself, much more than was required.

Every person possesses a positive as well as a negative side. The goal when it comes to the negative side is at first to become aware of this side, then accept it, understand why it is within you and then work on it.

An example: one of my negative traits is anger. I was working on it with the goal of dissolving this anger completely within me. My attitude was 'I must not get angry no matter what'. I spent months working on this trait, studying the patterns, its common causes and tried various meditations and techniques to let it go.

One day in my meditation, I got a message making me realize that the intention of trying to dissolve my anger was wrong and that instead, I must learn the meaning and purpose of this anger, and go deeper within myself to understand it and balance it.

These feelings of anger are originally a way to protect us, as a form of defence and also for sudden action. But unfortunately today it more commonly serves the need for people to feel powerful and dominant.

Aristotle said in his book *The Nicomachean Ethics*: 'Anybody can become angry – that is easy, but to be angry with the right person and to the right degree and at the right time and for the right purpose and in the right way – that is not within everybody's power and is not easy'.

The answer for me was to go deeper within my childhood and to study my family at a deeper level to understand the roots of my anger, and then to work on them. It is important to understand these concepts with the right state of mind in order to make progress on our spiritual journey.

The main lesson: making a soul mirror is not enough, you have to work on balancing yourself as well.

What happens when you regularly carry out introspection on yourself?

16. You will become more aware of your behavior, your emotions and emotional patterns in your daily life.

17. If you react negatively in a given situation, you will understand why you reacted in such a way, and also gain insights into the root cause of such reaction.

PART I: INTROSPECTION

18. You will learn about your subconscious behavior patterns and you will be able to see through situations that will prevent you from repeating the same mistakes again and again.

19. You will be more in control. Your emotions won't control you, you will control your emotions.

20. You will find more focus and stability in your life.

21. Introspection will enhance your listening skills. Once you learn to understand your behavior, you will discover that along with the understanding of the self comes the understanding of others, and an ability to easily understand people and their perspectives, biases and individual circumstances.

22. It will enhance your observation skills. You will be able to observe situations and people in a deeper, sharper way and with a greater understanding.

23. It will enhance your decision-making skills and diplomacy.

24. When you have a tough decision to make, use the introspection exercise and contemplate on the subject as a third person observer, fully aware and conscious of all negative traits of your personality which could misguide you. Do positive feelings of love, compassion, or devotion guide you towards your choice or are you being influenced by vanity, greed or pride? Introspection can make you aware of such influences which you might have been unaware of so far.

25. You will start healing your deepest wounds and would be in a position to help others to heal their wounds, to take them out of darkness and into the light.

26. You will learn to accept your true self and feel confident within your skin.

27. You will be able to apply the same observation skills you used on yourself to others in order to understand them and where they are coming from. If for example you are considering a business agreement with a person, your experience with the introspection exercise would help you decipher the person's motivations behind the agreement. It can help you to make better decisions when it comes to working with people.

The benefits from the efforts you make in this initial step of training today will last forever with you.

One question people often ask about the first step is how to be sure that the requirements for this initial step have been met so that they can move on to the next steps.

Answer: first of all you need to realize that unless you become aware of your true self, no matter how much knowledge you gain and how much intellectual vanity you are able to acquire, you will always lack the wisdom that comes from experience, and you will hurt yourself with jealousy by seeing others' progress.

A true seeker should dare to go deeper within himself, to face his inner demons and then when he is ready, to move ahead with complete dedication.

The answer to the question is, you will know that you have mastered the first step when you see the qualities I mentioned above in your behavior and in your daily life. When introspection becomes a habit, when awareness of your mind comes naturally to you, and when you have control over your mind – the 'monkey mind' – then you are free to move ahead with the next steps in your spiritual journey.

>In my opinion this exercise functions as a base and foundation for your future spiritual progress. It is truly *'The Beginning'*.

PART I: INTROSPECTION

3. Creating The Soul Mirrors – Ewen

Brief overview

The most basic way of creating the soul mirrors is to follow Bardon's IIH system using the three levels of Fire, Water, Air and Earth. Later on if you so wish you can build on this by organizing into categories as you see fit. We would prioritize that which is important for our person first – spirit, soul and body – to work in a harmonious way.

At the beginning, when creating the soul mirrors, the first introspection advised is that we set aside a time and fill the pages with everything that comes to mind for both white and negative mirrors. The next step should be that every day or evening we will fill in whatever we find in the moment or during contemplation. Continuous practice of this will help us find out more about ourselves and our elemental attributes.

However after having said this, in practice when starting out, you may find very quickly that these simple steps are not easily adhered to. At first the attributes may be recorded frivolously, usually only the black mirror negating the white. But soon you will find out that when days turn into weeks maybe one or two self-critiques will be recorded, that is even if you remember. Do not despair; this is all part of the journey and self-training. I have personally rewritten my Black and White mirrors, transferring them to new books many times, and making sure they are reflecting my current attributes accurately. Often during the transfer you will find negative attributes you have naturally corrected or a positive attribute that you have and is worth noting down.

Basic advice

There's always the problem for beginners to know which attributes belong to what element.

A practical way is to use the opportunity of rewriting the old book into a new book as a means of revising the feel of the attributes, for which really belongs to according to what you've read in IIH or other source materials. It is my own personal mistake to think that I could get every attribute down into its specific element in one day. Alhough it's a good way to start the book with that energy, you will find that naturally through time you will hone your understanding about the attributes and categorise them accordingly. In its very basic practice an attribute can be put into a single element. For example, saying : 'I don't like to share my donuts with others', you would think of being stingy. Say we would put in black mirror – earth.

Once we are used to this idea, we could then further break down what's the motivating factor of that statement. Say we broke it down to

1. fear of loss (scarcity) – earth (protection or preservation)

But also,

- Voracious eater – fire
- Emotional eating – water
- Antisocial – air

From here we can find the strongest motivating factor and be able to reorganise the statement in its correct element. If the feeling is having the same strength to two or more elements then we could put them in their respective place. With time and practice we will come to realise which is the correct category for each.

If you get the idea by now, you can go deeper contemplating the above the same way previously. Otherwise you can just keep it simple by putting it in one element and stop there.

The white soul mirror is equally important. It doesn't seem so because we use our strength all the time to the point we don't even know it's there, but we kind of know because we've been using it subconsciously! So why list it? Try it. You will be surprised to find hidden strengths which you want and be able to strengthen further. Most importantly the feeling in writing black and white is different. There is a feel of balance that comes with writing them. Besides, you will feel happier when doing so. It would be worrying if you don't.

PART I: INTROSPECTION

Unique ways for introspection

Apart from divination, the tarot cards are great for introspection as they are initially designed for it. Due to its multivalent and perfect nature, the tarot can quickly summon up key words, images, feelings and insights from within. One can divine with the cards where in our spiritual progress we are lacking or whatever area needs attention or improvement. There are numerous classes that teach on the subject of tarot. There are many types of decks and the most popular is the Rider-Waite-Smith deck. However, you should choose the one that you can relate with best as you can divine with any deck whether traditional or contemporary.

The tarot cards are readily available at your local mystic store or online and for a few dollars and a few days of shipping time you may possess one of the most powerful tools for spiritual progress.

One other way is to notice the people that you surround yourself with – or happen to be surrounded by. Long story short, we attract people of the same vibration. The more you are able to see your own elemental attributes, the more you will notice it in the people you are with, even if perhaps they are your colleagues and that they 'had to be there'.

For example, sometimes you feel you're next to the most stubborn person in the world and that you're the complete opposite and the most flexible. But take a step back and have a closer look and you will find more often than not that you have that stubbornness all along, perhaps not directly expressed but manifested in subtle different ways.

However more important is to be aware of your own actions or reactions towards this person as this will tell you of your own attributes. This is important information for introspection.

Personal reflections with introspection

You can see that from what I have written the significant value of introspection and what it will bring into your life. I can clearly see what motivates my actions and how easily I am led, or not led, into doing things. I am aware of where I am lacking and immediately change that element if it directly applies to my situation. I am also able to see others' negative elements at work, trying to pull me away from my own principles, and can see that they are frustrated when they cannot influence, and try many other ways to do so.

Although the beginning stage is about identifying attributes and categorizing their elements, we can still work on them immediately if it is needed to improve one's life.

Life experiences

I would love to be able to share a funny and entertaining experience relating to life-changing introspection but none comes to mind. So with a more melancholic undertone I will share an experience I had with a lady that led to my spiritual evolution.

I met her at a bar and she reminded me of my first. At first glance I saw the word 'trouble' written all over her. 'Just like the first' I thought to myself. But her type seems to keep coming back into my life as I've met a few before her. So I thought this time I'd stop fate dead in its tracks to find out why.

I agreed to pay to spend the night with her. But when the time came to be alone together, I chose only to lay in bed fully clothed; nothing happened that night save a few drinks and smokes. In my mind I knew this was different. I felt we met for a very different reason but not knowing what. She said I could stay the night. We slept with her in my arms. The morning sun broke in through the window but it was her dark grey-white curly and furry dog that had fully woken us. She had to go to work, I had to leave. I asked her to call me, she said yes. We kissed, I left. After that day, a year long personal spiritual journey with her started that made a journey with the mountain monks looks like a summer vacation in the Bahamas.

You name, it she had it – suicidal, self-mutilating, abused and cheated by ex, parents left her, child abused, schizophrenic bipolar, drug abuse, alcoholic and so on. I did everything I could to help her and try get her back on track. I knew I had stepped into a trap but I wanted to know how far would the rabbit hole go – what is it that fate wanted me to see from this? I wanted so desperately to find out, so I kept on going trying to 'save' her.

PART I: INTROSPECTION

In another way, I see it that Divine Providence has given me a chance to help someone. I promised Him that I would stay put no matter what for this chosen spirit of His. I would use what limited power I had to make it work for her. I tried everything – talking to her, motivating her, helping her, sending blessings, I spent all my time, energy and resources. Any average Joe knows it's a dead end. I near bankrupted myself. Even so, I was patient. I seldom argued with her but kept doing my 'duties' to 'save' her. I knew it was wrong in the most basic sense. But I tried to get through to her. I tried to get through to her spirit. I needed to see the truth, whatever it was.

Through the exhaustion and experience, finally I found what I was looking for. I found – me. I found deep humility. The elements and attributes that were so deep and that I never thought I'd have, surfaced. I found my greatest strength and faced my darkest shadow. I discovered how I was actually like her in many ways, but that side was hidden and buried underneath all those years of masking the self. I lifted common addictions and passions. Now I see past physical allure into spirit. I harmonize with constructive thoughts. Through her I catapult my fate into a new and beautiful direction.

Today I'm surrounded by people who are both beautiful on the inside and out. At times I'm not used to it as the change feels so sudden. It's like a boulder rolling down a hill so fast I'm trying to keep up with it. I found a workplace with a superior who is very caring and promotes harmony. My inner stability of my elements repels naturally those with elements which are inclined towards disharmony.

To finish my story, more happened after that but not much worth mentioning in terms of spirituality. After my elements were corrected naturally I felt it was time to end the journey. I remembered it like yesterday; I was on my computer when I came to a realisation of everything and it felt as if a weight had come off my shoulders. Everything was clear and finally I told her that my work was done and fate will look after her from then onwards. Sadly, through her friend, the last I heard she had carried on with her self-destructive ways; a spirit trapped inside herself. So the final conclusion? - Huh, it's the five of swords.

I do not in any way recommend anyone to go through what I have. This was purely a personal journey. However, I do hope one can see how I derive the method and importance of introspection from one of my own personal experience. That through real world experience and reviewing of the elements you will come to grips the elements which are in yourself and finally find your true spirit.

I would like to thank Divine Providence for providing me with the experience and being able to share it with you all. I hope this will light a spark in someone's heart and that it will be found inspirational. Thank you for giving me the opportunity to express myself and may the blessings of Divine Providence shine bright upon all.

PART I: INTROSPECTION

4. Balancing The Humors – A Traditional Approach to the Work of The Soul Mirrors – Martin Faulks

In this article I am going to write about the elemental balance from a historical perspective. The idea that part of our inner quest is to balance the elements of earth, water, air and fire is a prominent feature in Hermetic traditions, but we also see the same concept powerfully expressed within other western lineages, oriental paths and yogic disciplines. Sometimes the phrasing is slightly different or the perspective varies slightly, for example whether you are balancing your Doshas using Ayurvedic medicine or balancing your meridians or chakras. The idea that these forces must be brought into full expression and harmony is very much a part of the preliminary training in almost every path of awakening undertaken. The concept that someone should or would balance out their inner elements is really very ancient. Some people even believe that it dates back to the earliest Egyptian medicine. But firm evidence only appears in writing in the Hellenic tradition in about the fifth century BC. The pre-socratic philosopher Empedocles really did a wonderful job in establishing the concept that the whole of existence was made from the four elements and this started to have an influence on medical practices.

Now you may have heard of the legendary doctor Hippocrates who concluded that just as all things were made of the elements, so too was man. It seemed logical that when this man consumed food this was digested and broken down into Four Humors or inner elements. This idea had a great influence and Hippocrates' writings and practices spread throughout the world. It is probably through his tradition that the Hermetic path took on this idea because we know that the Hippocratic practices were very popular in ancient Alexandria during the time the Hermetic writings were recorded. If we carry on this tradition we see that it becomes analyzed, systematized and perfected in great detail within the Roman Empire. One Roman doctor called Galen who lived in the second century AD wrote a lot on the subject. This spread to the Arab world and all over the Roman Empire.

The basic idea is that we all have natural tendencies toward different temperaments brought about by these humors. When we eat food our digestion breaks it back down into the four elements.

The four humors which are the essential elements in the body are:

Yellow Bile – Choleric: The fire element circulating within you

Blood – Sanguine: The air element circulating within you

Phlegm – Phlegmatic: The water element circulating within you

Black Bile – Melancholic: The earth element circulating within you

Some of these words have associations different from their modern meaning, so it is important not to confuse them. For example, when ancient texts refer to blood they are focusing on the air element. This is connected to what we would call blood and of course we know oxygen is carried in blood. However, the meaning is slightly different, since it is the idea that it is the circulation of that air element we are focusing on rather than just the physical blood.

Similarly when phlegm is mentioned, someone with a predominance of water would have more phlegm in the modern sense, but phlegm relates to the actual water within the system.

So your digestion may take a predominance of one of these elements out of the food naturally and you may be more responsive to one humor. What you eat has a very strong influence, so if you eat food that is of one element that will have a significant effect on you. In the same way, what you do, what you see, and what influences are upon you have an effect on your humors inside – the air you breathe, the people you see, the job and hobbies you have. That will change the balance of the humors; if you do a lot of fiery things you will become more fiery; if you do a lot of calming things you will become more like water. The same of course is true of the other elements. These elements mix within you and this 'crasis' or mixing process is a very important thing. If it mixes well, eucrasia, even though you may have a predominance of the element, you are in control; the expression is healthy

PART I: INTROSPECTION

and all works. This good mixing leads to a good mind and a good life. If we have bad mixing, dyscrasia, the mixing isn't right; we have too much of an element or things are not working quite right and illness will result.

Everyone has a temperament based on one of these humors. If you had a predominance of black bile you would be melancholic; if you had a predominance of phlegm you would be phlegmatic. A predominance of chorea or yellow bile would make you choleric. A predominance of blood would make you sanguine. Some of these terms are used in the modern day, normally to express a particular temperament. Now the expression of the different humors was also seen to change with other factors. It was seen as being very affected by age.

A new-born baby is more dominated by the air element and thus more sanguine. Young people would probably have more yellow bile, and probably be more fiery. As time goes on one would see this change. When one matures in life one would start to be a bit more earthly. This change continues as our life progresses and eventually in old age we become more watery.

- Blood was the humor of spring, passion, air and childhood

- Yellow bile belonged to summer, anger, fire and youth

- Black bile was linked to a sluggish personality, autumn, earth and adulthood

- Phlegm was associated with winter, melancholy, water and old age

These humors were also affected by many other factors. Digestion was seen to take place within the various organs. So the spleen would produce the fiery yellow bile, the liver the earthy melancholy black bile, the heart the air enthused blood and the lungs the watery phlegm.

So the health of these organs would make a big difference to how much of that element you can extract from your food and how influenced you were by these elements around you. Things were not just set, so as you went through your life the balance of your elements would change.

It was seen during childhood that you would probably have more air, so you would be more sanguine. As you grew into youth fire would express itself more, through a more choleric temperament. As you became more mature, black bile, the humor of earth would become stronger, making you become more melancholy. As you reached old age the phlegmatic aspect would be expressed as the water element became stronger.

The Humors were not just seen as affecting the workings of the body but also those of the mind.

- Blood – brings feelings of happiness, enthusiasm, humor, optimism and success

- Phlegm – encourages flexibility, emotion, lethargy, selfishness, devotion and dedication, sensitivity and sentimentality

- Yellow Bile – provokes ambition, bravery, a call for justice, passion, anger, boldness, envy, irritability, jealousy and courage

- Black Bile – induces melancholy, contemplation, prudence, caution, pessimism and persistence

Even the time of day would make a difference. So one who was prone to a predominance of a certain element may find that it expresses itself more strongly at the time of that element. One who was an air personality would feel this more in the morning. One who was more fiery would feel this at midday. An earthy person would feel that express itself in the afternoon. We would also see water come forth in the evening of the day, just as we saw in the evening of life. Similarly the different seasons would have an elemental expression also, spring relating to air, summer being fire, autumn associated with earth, and winter linked to water.

This is very important because it helps us to see and identify the elemental balance within a person. The elements all have their own qualities and these express themselves within the person through their predominance. So someone who has a lot of fire has the qualities of hot and dry and if their mix is right, if everything is all good they may be warm and resilient to the cold and their body would be resistant to anything that would be a negative influence of water. They would be full of action and ambitious. Everything

PART I: INTROSPECTION

fiery would be expressing itself just right. If however the balance was wrong you would see them lose control and express anger. This heat and dryness would express itself in the body somewhere. So perhaps they would be prone to fevers, dryness or rashes of the skin. When you talk to them they may say that it is worse in summer. They may tell you that they find their spleen expresses discomfort. They may tell you that it is worse at midday.

So by knowing when these different humors express themselves – as I have listed – will help the doctor or practitioner identify what needs to be brought into balance. But how would the Hippocratic doctor or practitioner of Ancient Hermeticism, who understood these teachings in Ancient times, bring about a balance in these humors?

Well, they would understand that although many different factors influence the balance in humans, the most powerful and influential factor is the food that is eaten. By looking at what the person ate and how they ate, they would be able clearly to see the elements expressing themselves. So their understanding would be that people chose the type of food according to their predominant element. So one who has the predominance of choleric would like spicy or bitter food; they want it hot and want it dry and eat with great speed and vigor. One who had a sanguine temperament would have a predominance of air and eat with the same kind of enthusiasm that someone would put into words looking for the small details. They would be a connoisseur looking for hot and moist and loving the sweet food. One who had a phlegmatic temperament were very watery, they would want cold moist food. They would like to eat fruit and finger buffets. They would eat with an ongoing gentle flow a loving salty food in particular. One who was of the melancholy temperament would want to eat to express their predominance of earth, wanting cold and dry food, sour if possible. They would eat wishing to simply consume for the sake of consuming with a solid ongoing repetitive plodding nature. Changing what the person eats would change them. We have heard the saying 'you are what you eat'. In ancient times this was taken in a far more literal way. If you wanted to help someone balance their elements you would bring around the opposite to their expression of appetite.

So to illustrate this approach, let me explore an example. Let us imagine that someone we knew described certain symptoms which they were concerned about. Perhaps they found themselves lacking energy, maybe they felt depressed and withdrawn from society. You could then look towards other symptoms. Could it be that this person is expressing a melancholy temperament – a predominance of earth in other ways? Perhaps they were always cold, perhaps they had dryness of the eyes. Perhaps their symptoms were worse during the afternoon. In traditional Greek medicine we would look to the influences of the earth signs upon them, Taurus, Virgo and Capricorn. We might see when the planet Saturn was having a strong influence and see if this brought about a worsening of their symptoms. Maybe we would look at the balance and health of their organs. Does the liver show signs of over-work?

Once we have established this we can have a look at their eating habits. It would be probable that they were eating very simple plain earthy food. Sometimes we would see some attempt at balance that was not working. So we might find that there were certain times when this repetitive, plain, earthy food and lack of appetite suddenly burst into an opposite tendency. Maybe you would see them have strong cravings that suddenly appear, that is something full of the air element. Maybe they would have lots of bread or a fizzy drink – something that possesses this air quality. What we need to do is to look at bringing about an ongoing consumption of food which represents the balancing elements. They need foods that correspond to air, not in bursts but as a predominance. We seek to bring a hot/moist quality to everything they consume. We look at the law of analogy to see what we can use to bring the quality of air within them, whether it be leaves that blow in the wind that are edible, or flowers which can be consumed, something that would return this air inward. Then and only then we would have established this balancing diet. We then look to other ways to bring about that balance. This would of course involve things that would help the heart, which is of course the organ of air. Influences which would inspire their mind – which brings about this sanguine temperament. We would make sure they were up in the morning and that they spent time in places of air and perhaps time with others who are of the more airy nature. Maybe we would prescribe specific exercises relating to the air element, such as breathing exercises or singing. All this would be based on the firm foundations of the correct diet; the elements in their most material form are going into the body; sweet foods and hot moist foods; the foods that grow in spring; the foods which are of the

PART I: INTROSPECTION

air element and contain air within them. This would bring about better blood circulation. It would help bring about the good mix that is eucrasia within a person. This in turn would bring about a more balanced mind, and this balanced mind would bring about better judgements and a better life.

Once we have established that, after this balance we start to see the symptoms disappear and the person starts to find their energy return and naturally gain more of an appetite. We may even see symptoms such as the dryness of the eyes disappear. Once this regime is perfected we need to remember the ebbs and flows of the different temperaments throughout the day and throughout the year. Knowing that because the earth element is more predominant at times in that person's life would mean that we may have to adapt their diet slightly in order to armour them in events related to such things. So during the autumn, you would like to make sure that they have the greatest regime of balance in place.

This example I hope will express a fundamental approach using this philosophy enough that anyone who reads this will be able to apply it to their lives and begin through contemplation and application to unlock the mystery of these humors within themselves. I hope this has been of value to those wishing to learn the inner wisdom of elements from the past.

5. Mirror of The Soul – Angel of God

To create a mirror of the soul is not an easy task for sure, because it deals with the greatest mystery to humans – greater than complicated arithmetic equations, scientific hypotheses and so on. Here we deal with man and who he is.

Here we deal with hypotheses about ourselves; we deal with what we think we are and we write that down. Amateurishly we write 'I am Strong, so I am more fire element or even earth'. This is where the person is miserably mistaken. When faced with introspection, Plato said 'I only know that I know nothing' and the wise men of Delphi answered 'And that is why you are the wisest among men'. To think that he knows, to think that he knows, to think that he is, this indeed is a tremendous mistake.

Do you really want to know yourself? For that there are not many secrets. Just look at how much time you spend with yourself and how much you spend for the benefit of others. It is simple. For if you spend most of your time with yourself, you are selfish. Now, if you spend it with others, you are altruistic. Simple.

But the ego insists on justifying the unjustifiable by arguing: 'But shouldn't this be magic advice? Shouldn't what I'm reading lead me to the highest cosmic powers? Shouldn't I approach angels and geniuses of other dimensions?'

Of course, but first I want to take away those dark shadows that tuck you in your bed, that watch over you day and night and that many and many times guide your thoughts and actions. If I understand, it is the devil that guides you, because of course it is the devil. Even if you think that it is the angels who have said 'Stay at home and rest. Forget the one who is hungry and in pain. The important thing is that you rest, isn't it? Do you really think you will be able to progress in the gift that is the initiation into Hermeticism written by one of the most helpful beings of this planet, Bardon? At home and in total omission? Do you really believe that the greatest mysteries will be given to you, just to you? A beauty for a selfish one?'

PART I: INTROSPECTION

Now your mind might be thinking 'But this has nothing to do with magic, here it only has lessons in morality.' But of course human 'genius' has morality. Not only morality, but ethics, virtues, work and effort, indispensable qualities, for anyone who longs for true power.

So get up and start to be useful. Visit the sick, clarify the ignorant, take the pain of the one who suffers, help without wanting anything in return, but do something. Bardon in his infinite wisdom and great capacity decided to give you the lesson of writing down your defects and virtues and from there to understand something, but it seems that you like to be alone on the surface ... You like to imagine yourself as a being full of all virtues and blessings, and many times those who read even think that you are an authentic incarnate angel! He only came to teach and set an example ... Poor thing ...

The power, the maximum power, the gift to speak 'It rains' and it rains and to say 'Stop' and the rain stops, this is only given to those who truly know themselves, who know until the last drop of evil within themselves vanishes, who have acquired self-knoweldge until the last shadow that lives within them-selves has been dominated. He conquered all illusions, he conquered human passions, he conquered the darkness that inhabits his heart, he conquered all egoism and omission that permeates his being.

Do you really want to know yourself? Do you really want to know who you are? Look at yourself, but look sincerely. Remember that while you rest, while you are fed up, others starve, others are in pain, others weep.

And if you still insist on thinking that all this I say has nothing to do with magic, my friend ... There is no greater magic than to make hope shine in the heart that no longer sees light, to make a smile appear where there is only sadness. The coming of Christ was not to multiply loaves and fish and fill the stomachs, or even show that he could walk on the waters or heal diseases. The greatest miracle he did was to rekindle hope in the hearts of billions – was to remind people that life is more than matter and that there is eternal life afterwards.

I do not expect you to understand my words, but do assess whether you really want to know yourselves and progress in Hermeticism. Begin to be sincere with yourself, to be kind to yourself and with your brother. You accuse, judge and condemn, and lie to yourself. Grow up. Men start acting like men. Women start acting like women. Grow up. Until when will you continue to act like children?

If you have courage and follow my advice, know that only IF you really know each other, will you have the power to have everything you want. It is a hard task and involves much suffering, but it is worth it. Someday you will look back and your hearts will be filled with joy in being able to say 'Today I am good. No more of that selfish crap that I was once'. And that day, my friends, tears of joy will fill your eyes and the trumpets from heaven will be blown because you will know each other. You answered.

PART I: INTROSPECTION

6. A FAVORITE ACTIVITY OF SATURN – WILLIAM R. MISTELE

[Editor's note: This piece is an excerpt from a longer essay by William Mistele entitled *Saturn Spirit Evocation*. The full essay can be found on his website.[1]]

Some individuals have a magical will which is so powerful and hostile it would easily interfere with others' spiritual development if given free reign. These individuals are, let us say, on probation from the Judges of Saturn and they are assigned inner plane case workers or probation officers who watch them closely. If they use the dark side of their will, as Bardon mentions, there are demonic beings near at hand who will make every effort to take control of them.

One of the roles Saturn plays in astrology is to take away. Saturn makes transits and says, 'Time's up. You have had your chance to grow, to develop, to solve your problems, and to learn to be free. You have had the chance to make a contribution to your world. Now the resources I gave you are no longer available.' But Saturn does something even worse. Due to actions of a former lifetime or in a current situation, Saturn will curse someone by binding that individual within a tormenting spiritual and psychic isolation. It does not matter how many people they know or who know them. They are placed within an astral abyss.

Furthermore, what is so Saturnian about this judgment is that Saturn will not give a single clue as to what the person must do to undo the curse. In the Arthurian Legend, King Arthur, with his life at stake, had to answer within one year the riddle; 'What do women want most from men?' And his friend Gawain helped him out and in so doing undid a curse on another individual. But there is no such help for those cursed by Saturn.

The reason for this is that Saturn is the guardian of conscience. An individual who has abused spiritual and magical power has damaged his own conscience. Consequently, on their own initiative they must engage in

---
1 Specifically at the following link - http://williammistele.com/saturn.html

prolonged introspection – a favorite activity of Saturn – in order to recreate what they have destroyed in themselves. In other words, they have to figure out on their own what the disharmony is and what they have to do to make things right.

Excuses, anger, resentment, revenge, blame, hatred, animosity, greed, corruption – these must be put aside completely and a new individual must be created, an individual who chooses to be free of all negative influence. The will required to accomplish this is often greater in magnitude than anything the individual has exerted before. Yet it often requires the most severe and depressing of life circumstances to get them even to consider that they are responsible for the situations they have fallen into. Only when they see that all they have can be taken away again and again do they begin to start listening to their conscience or wondering why they have not had the wisdom to avoid their present situation

PART I: INTROSPECTION

7. SOUL MIRROR EXERCISES – ILYAS RAHHALI

Now about some ways to make the soul mirror exercise easier, or looking at it from another point of view, we can use what I choose to call the 'branching technique'. It is a top down technique where we go from bigger ideas and dividing them into smaller, more specific ones. Imagine the topic of negative traits as a huge and thick tree. This massive tree has multiple levels, each having multiple branches, and each branch multiple leaves. We can think of the levels as big areas of character traits. For instance, health, social interactions, habits, beliefs, religion, hobbies and all big, high level categories you can think of.

Then come branches for each level. Let's take health for example; we can divide it into hygiene, nutrition, sleep and many others. Then comes the level of leaves. Here you take each subcategory and find all things you do, think, believe that are negative and relative to that subcategory. Let's take sleep for the example. You can have traits of sleeping late, waking up late (yes, it's two different traits even if they are linked), using your phone too much before sleep, picking up the phone first thing in the morning, and any other behaviors you believe are negative that relate to sleep.

You can supplement this practice with the following variant. If you're doing your soul mirrors again past Step Two of IIH, you can even make it more fun, by using your plastic imagination skills. So, what you might find fun to do is for each of the categories, or even leaves, you can write or imagine a perfect scenario, how ideally you would like to behave in a certain situation related to the category in question. And then meditate on what's stopping you from actually doing that ideal scenario. The idea behind this is, instead of just thinking and waiting for some traits to spontaneously pop up in your head, you create situations and scenarios which are familiar to your brain, so it's easier for it to find the traits. We must remember that our brains function by associations, so in a familiar situation, your brain is more prone to remembering a bad trait or behavior.

Let me illustrate this variant with an example. Imagine and write down your ideal productive day, from the moment you wake up until the moment you fall asleep. Detail which activities you do with timestamps. Then reflect on your actual daily routine. What's different from your ideal day? Why is it so? You might find for example that ideally, you want to wake up at 5 a.m. However, you often find yourself waking up at 8:30 instead. Why is that? List all the reasons you can think of as traits on your black soul mirrors or leaves on your tree.

Another example might be that you imagine your ideal relationship with your partner or friend, boss, family member or even stranger. Write down how you'd like to behave and put what you're not doing in the black soul mirror.

Similarly, you should put all the behaviors that match your ideal on your white soul mirror.

You do this process for all levels, branches and leaves, and before you know it you have a hundred traits or more. What seemed like an impossible task at first, when you were just sitting down and trying to randomly brainstorm character traits, have been made extremely easy just by the fact of organizing and dividing.

The work is not done yet; you can still divide more. How precisely you want to go down the dividing part is really up to you and your introspective abilities, which will become honed and improved as you do this exercise. How do we divide more than that? By asking the simple question 'why?' for each of these traits. That's because one trait can be caused by many factors and other traits. This asking 'why?' exercise will make it way easier to do the elemental correspondences, because as we see you'll know exactly what is causing such behavior or trait to settle within you and to arise. Let me illustrate with an example. Let's take the sleeping late trait for example. Ask yourself 'Why am I sleeping late?'. Meditate over the question for some minutes and try being aware next time it's evening and you want to go to sleep, why do you feel resistance and pushing the time to later.

You might find for example that as you go sleep, you notice your phone on the bed table, and picture it as you lie down. And before you know it two hours have passed. The underlying trait here might be laziness and apathy – depending on what you do on your phone, I supposed here you're browsing social media or playing a game. It can be lethargy, it can be fear of missing out and so on. It can also be a combination of these traits, in which

PART I: INTROSPECTION

case, you separate each to a different entry in your soul mirror. That is because the trigger is different, and the trigger is what you should be working on when you root out the trait, not the surface symptom or behavior. The trigger also is the indication of what element is causing the trait. As such, you might for your example delay going to sleep because of lethargy and fear of missing out. You might label the first in earth or water element, and the second to air element.

Don't be afraid also to not label elements correctly. As with the first two steps, you don't yet have direct exposure and real experience of the elements – in the hermetic sense, not the physical one. So, you might not be sure which trait belongs to which element. But Bardon says it's alright if you miss the classification of some traits; just go with what you feel. And if you really need a starting idea, go on reading Bill Mistele's writings on elemental spirits and the elements. He describes them so well that you'll start instinctively knowing which element the trait belongs to.

Another pleasant side-benefit of doing the soul mirror exercise is that you'll see your self-awareness and introspection skills go through the roof. You'll notice that during everyday tasks or interactions with other people, you'll start labeling your actions automatically as 'this is bad, I don't need to do this'; 'why did I say such mean thing?'; 'can I spend the time I'm doing this activity better?/is doing this activity really beneficial to me?' and other introspective and self-assessing comment you maybe weren't doing before.

After some time, you might want to sit at night before sleeping and grab your introspection notebook. You'll start looking back into your day. Then from the events of that day, choose some that you find contain unwholesome acts of body, speech or mind, and see if their corresponding trait already exists in your soul mirror. Do not forget to do the same for wholesome acts as well. You might also check how much mindfulness and awareness of your state of mind you had during these events, and track your progress on the way of purifying the soul. After some practice, this will serve as a positive reinforcement, as you'll start realizing that in some events of your day, your actual behavior is totally different from before starting the purifying of soul practice, and much closer to the ideal one you have imagined in the previously mentioned exercise.

This was my experience regarding the soul mirror exercises. I also find myself wanting to do it again when my introspective skills improve to a new threshold, as the new mirrors are more accurate, better formulated and analyzed and also with better elemental correspondence.

You'll find your soul mirrors to be your best friend, and in the same way that you use a physical mirror to track your working out progress and admire your new fit and beautiful body, you'll be using your soul mirror to track your personality change progress and admire your soul becoming more charming, beautiful and pleasant.

PART I: INTROSPECTION

8. The Second Level of Introspection – Ray del Sole

We all know the first level of introspection, which Bardon teaches in IIH. Here we follow the long-term aim to balance and refine our personality. The second level of introspection is also about reflection of yourself but with the focus on your present situation:

- How is your present state?

- How do you feel?

- Do you feel vital, balanced, good, successful, inspired?

- Or do you feel stressed, overburdened, exhausted?

- Do you suffer?

- How can you improve your well-being?

- How can you maintain your well-being?

- What do you need to change in your attitude for more balance, more vitality, more happiness?

In fact, these are vital questions and quite often we are too busy with external duties, tasks and problems to check on ourselves, to check how we feel, what we need, if all is fine or bad or in need of changes.

For example, how can you be successful, vital and happy when you suffer from too many burdens, too much stress while lacking positive energy resources? This cannot work. Only when you return into a state of lightness, of joy of life, of vitality, then you can experience the good things in life.

In conclusion, problems are not only outside but they are also inside of us, anchored. And both are connected. Change yourself and your world will change. Change your world and you will change.

EQUIPOISE: INSIGHTS INTO FOUNDATIONAL ASTRAL TRAINING

Today there are many people who are completely overburdened, in part with very old things, old emotions, but also with family issues, spiritual issues, and certainly business issues. Even if you are powerful like Hercules, you do not need to bear all the heaviness of the world and you do not need to feel responsible for countless people and their problems.

It is wise to be satisfied with your own package of lessons and burdens, to work on them and not to take additional stuff from others as spiritual people often do. There is no real sense in sacrificing yourself. It is better to celebrate the joy of life and to honor in this way our Creator. We all have a right to our own happiness.

Practically seen – it makes sense to do the introspection II on a regular basis, maybe once a week to check if you are okay, if things and relationships in your life are good or if there is a need for changes. And if there is a need for changes, you should realize them as soon as possible. In this regard also be aware that your state of well-being has effects on all people in contact with you, your family, friends, co-workers, clients, etc. So when everyone takes care of himself then all will be happy and fine. And if burdens are spread in a good way then they are also good to bear.

We all need to be in a good state of balance, vitality and power.

PART I: INTROSPECTION

9. The Unveiling of Introspection – Tamoken

In ancient Greece, the temple of Apollo at Delphi greeted all seekers with the inscription of "Know Thyself." In Franz Bardon's *Initiation into Hermetics*, we are prescribed many methods to not only come to know ourselves, but also to gain the ability to change ourselves for the better. To any serious seeker, introspection is an important step on the path of spiritual ascension. Shortcomings may bring you to your knees, and your strengths may keep you spiritually protected and fortified. You will come to know yourself beyond a list of traits. You may discover who you were in previous incarnations and your true nature in the spiritual planes. As blasphemous as it may sound, I believe character transformation through step one and step two in *Initiation into Hermetics'* Magical Schooling of the Soul in and of itself could stand on its own as a personal development tool. I'll discuss the creation and refinement of soul mirrors, the influence of traits upon our lives, applying oneself to character transmutation, deep seated healing from soul work, and taking these tools to further improve our lives. This article is for anyone with a preliminary understanding of Franz Bardon's work. Thus, we begin with the list of character traits for our white and black soul mirrors.

I suggest initially listing at least fifty traits for each soul mirror. Throughout the years, you will add on more and update your mirrors many times, but this is a good start. If you are stretching your imagination to obtain more than twenty traits for each mirror, then muster self-application to reflect, research, and identify the most subtle nuances within you. The exercises in *Initiation into Hermetics* have us accessing parts of ourselves that are likely in a state of atrophy or simply never developed. If you're challenged with creating your soul mirrors, then from the get-go are you fortunate – throughout The Practice of Magic in *Initiation into Hermetics* we must strengthen our capacity to develop inner resources to successfully continue in the practice.

For creating the initial black and white soul mirror, there are quickly identifiable character traits we can pull into our awareness. These are words like happiness, sadness, joy, anger, frustration, humor, jealousy, kindness, etc.

EQUIPOISE: INSIGHTS INTO FOUNDATIONAL ASTRAL TRAINING

Consider these commonplace descriptive terms and determine if they apply to you. Take out a thesaurus and peruse through the words. Recall an entire day and all the states you experienced. In this day and age, you can look up a list of character traits online, scanning through the suggestions, and determine if they are fitting. Also strive to discover your character traits through quiet contemplation. Take note as new character traits reveal themselves. Add them to your black and white soul mirrors. The first draft of your soul mirrors will be an indicator of your current level of spiritual maturity and self-knowledge. Your soul mirrors are a reflection of the energies active, or dormant, within you. Interested in scrying? Well here you are scrying into your soul, gaining direct sight into the workings of your inner spheres.

My first set of soul mirrors had about fifty traits on each side. Fifteen years later, I currently have two hundred and sixty traits for each mirror. Soul mirror work is the door through which you'll find what energies work through your being, for better or for worse. As Bardon states, "In our abode, which is our body and soul, we must find our way about at all times." [2] As you do your inner work, you'll discover more subtle energies expressing themselves in you. This is important, knowing what energies are transpiring within you. The most subtle of energies unchecked could cause havoc in one's spiritual life. Over time, I also found that I could identify and appreciate mores subtle energies that are contained in more comprehensive words, for example, words like churlish, capricious, precocious and brazen. Improving one's vocabulary to include the use of lesser used, but more descriptive or concise words can articulate nuanced traits that everyday vernacular might not fully capture.

Even if one was not engaged in magical development, the quality and quantity of one's traits do change over the course of time. This is due to varying circumstances, karma, and life experiences exposing us to energies and situations that bring up different energies within us. Maybe you were popular in high school, so you never experienced jealousy until your first job out of college. Then you watched in confusion and dismay as the "nerd" was promoted and you were not. A trait you might not have identified initially can

---

[2] Franz Bardon, *Initiation into Hermetics* (Salt Lake City, UT: Merkur Publishing, Inc., 2001), page 69.

PART I: INTROSPECTION

reveal itself as an influential trait during a later event in life. Then, the unfolding of life has provided you a new trait to be cognizant of.

When you are ready to begin transmuting a character, initially seek out the negative trait that either is the most intense or one that is approachable for you. If you start with your strongest negative trait and become overwhelmed, select a trait less intense. While these exercises do take time, it is important to see gradual progress. One function of the soul mirror work is to allow us to safely proceed to further steps, so we do eventually need to address our stronger negative traits, and ideally sooner rather than later. As you may be aware, magical work further activates the energies already latent within you, including the negative ones. This is how many magical practitioners get a head bigger than a hot air balloon – by not having done the work to address their black mirror. For negative traits that are completely saturating, you have many tools from Bardon with which you can fervently apply yourself. Prayer can also be of great assistance. A month or two wrestling with a specific demon is well worth a lifetime of relief and freedom. Some negative traits can be banished in a matter of weeks. Some may take months or years.

Since the soul mirror work is so effective in transforming our lives, these tools could be their own practice in the name of personal development. While I would not promote this to aspiring Bardonist magicians, since it leads to one-sided development, I want to go more into why I would even make such a suggestion. True magical equilibrium, health and harmony are requirements for genuine magical ascent. Magical ascent is achieved by working on the spirit, soul and body simultaneously. However, what if one does not have the capacity for true magical ascension in this lifetime, but simply desires to get their spiritual house in order and tackle the negativity in their soul?

During the process of transmuting negative traits, coupled with psychic insight, I began to discover my karmic footprint. Let me give you a couple theoretical examples: Have a hard time trusting others? Maybe you gave your heart away and were betrayed by a lover in a past life. Fearful of swimming and boats? Maybe you had been lost at sea. Positive and negative traits are often deeply rooted in our distant past. These traits become charged from experiences in previous incarnations. This is why I previously mentioned some negative traits may take months or years to resolve. For example, whilst in the process of transmuting anger, you activate the related past experiences where the anger was charged and fed. Through applying the tools for character transmutation, you are simultaneously working through any related karmic healing, unbeknownst to you. Although the initial cause of the negative trait started in another life, these experiences are still influencing you, and soul mirror work allows you to begin correcting them in the here and now.

In the several aspects of soul mirror work, such as identifying character traits, balancing elements, or even healing past karma, you can also cultivate new traits that will improve your life condition. Perhaps equanimity would serve you well. Or charisma. Or assertiveness. Carefully observe your current life. Take the opportunity to continue using the tools you've gained to not only balance your soul mirrors, but to make you a better person. While we can balance out the traits currently active within us, we may also find ourselves lacking the right traits to master our current life situation. Luckily, as an aspiring magician you have the tools to cultivate new positive traits. Our goal may be to advance to Bardon's second and third books, *The Practice of Magical Evocation* and *The Key to the True Kabbalah*, but already in the first two steps of *Initiation into Hermetics* we have ample tools to radically transform our lives.

In reflecting upon soul mirror work, we see that our character traits have already established patterns within and without ourselves. Laziness and complacency may be holding you back from new opportunity. Ambition and egoism may create an isolating life. Just as neural pathways form in our brains and can be consciously influenced, so can the patterns in our soul be rearranged through consciously working on our soul mirrors. As prescribed in *Initiation into Hermetics*, autosuggestion, magic of water, will power, and the loading and magnetizing of food are effective tools to alter the elemental composition within you. By doing so, you also alter the rhythm and the operation of cause and effect upon your life. As a stand-alone practice, the soul mirror work can allow you to work through deep seated karma and restricted ways of being, thus saving yourself from the pains and troubles of such things in future incarnations or spheres. Activities like autosuggestion and applying will power against one's shortcomings are already common-known tools for personal development.

PART I: INTROSPECTION

However, my hope is that all sincere students of *Initiation into Hermetics* will find their way through patient and diligent practice, simultaneously working on the development of the body, soul and spirit. Introspection opens the portal to deeper self-realization and genuine magical development. It allows us to refine our being and discern that which we are and that which we are not. In a world where so many identities and projections exist, our soul mirrors show us the raw materials that truly influence us. We can settle into self-knowledge, but also take up the tools to chisel our soul into a true work of art. Magical development allows us to manifest our full potential, yet we must meet ourselves in the present, and not fret about the what lies ahead in the future.

10. With Great Power Comes Great Responsibility – Gregory Jeremiah Touw Ngie Tjouw

My name is Gregory Jeremiah Touw Ngie Tjouw. I am 32 years old, of Surinamese descent and live with my family in Amsterdam. A while ago I was approached through Facebook by Stephen Smith asking if I thought it would be a good idea to participate in a collective project to benefit the Best Friends Animal Society.

I have two cats and an adopted dog from Romania, so I thought this was a very nice gesture to help animals. I have been a student in IIH for almost nine years now. I will do my best to write about my experience.

I come from a family of three children and I am the oldest. My father left the family when I was three years old; my brother and my sister had just been born. My mother raised us alone and that has not been easy. If my mother had to work late in the weekend, we would usually stay with my grandmother, a sweet old woman who has devoted her life to Jehovah. We were always free to play and watch television but the Bible was always read aloud. I always liked the lyrics and listened carefully. Yet at a young age I realized that there was much more than the word of God. I felt that there was more than being 'human' and living in a world where you go to school to find a job, maybe get married and have children. To be honest, I always felt myself worldly strange and different from most people. My favorite cartoon was *Spiderman* with Peter Parker in the lead, who is bitten by a spider and has super powers. After a fight his uncle Ben Parker tells Peter that with great power comes great responsibility. These are words that have always stayed with me and only have meaning for me today.

I never really knew what I wanted to be when I grew up. At the age of thirteen I started my first job as a dishwasher in a Chinese restaurant and earned quite well. With that money I could buy nice things and help my mother. At a young age I had to deal with a purchase addiction. As soon as I got paid, I bought clothes and spent the money on going out. I come from a neighborhood where there was a lot of crime. Most people had a job but did something besides to earn extra money. I saw it happen and before I knew it I

PART I: INTROSPECTION

was at night in a garage stealing scooters with some friends after work. We did not get exhausted because we made good money from this.

From scooters we switched to motorbikes and every now and then we were caught by the police and received a community service order. That did not scare us and we started to concern ourselves with drugs and all sorts of other things. Often I rode my motorcycle to a quiet place where I would sit and look around on my own. I looked at the sky, I saw the stars and I wondered what the meaning was; why am I here? I have experienced many supernatural things. Often I saw people who could not see other people next to me or I had dreams of visiting other places with other beings. Before falling asleep I also often heard the voice of a woman calling my name. These events made me more spiritual than religious.

In 2010 my father was murdered in Suriname. He himself was in a criminal circle and this was a reckoning. After his cremation, I withdrew from the people and my aunt's husband came to stand beside me. He embraced me and told me that as long as I did not do what my father did he would give me everything; as long as I did not live as he had lived he would give me everything. I remember that I started crying. A few days after my father's cremation we drove deep into the forest and went to visit a lady. My uncle told us that she would wash us spiritually. This was not very strange for us because this happens a lot in our culture, often on New Year's Day, for all the bad things in the previous year. After the washing my sister, brother and I stood next to each other. The lady stood in front of us and smoked a cigar. She took a sip of the drink my uncle had brought her and stared at us with piercing eyes. At one point she looked at the sky and her posture changed. Her facial expression changed and she said my name. After saying my name I saw my father. The lady stood before us but I saw my father. Her way of talking and moving were the way my father would.

On that sad day I experienced something very beautiful, a great event, and my question was answered. There is more than the human eye can see. There is more than what is learned in schools.

After the death of my father, I became more spiritual and began to realize that I had a strong mind. If I wanted something and thought about it, I got it. If I wrote a song as a rapper and spoke about a certain something in my text, this happened. But how could I know more about this, how could I further develop this?

A year after my father's death, I met a man named Ed. Ed looked very simple, no expensive clothes or shoes, but this man was a walking encyclopedia. He knew everything about music and spirituality.

We often talked about the meaning of life and one day he wrote something on a piece of paper and gave it to me. I took it and read what it said. Franz Bardon - *Initiation into Hermetics*. 'When you are finished with work you have to buy this book', he said. 'This book will answer all your questions and give meaning to your life.'

After work, I hurried to the bookstore and bought the book.

I felt a kind of tension and joy. When I arrived home I started reading and couldn't stop. The words I read touched me inside and it was as if I had always known this. Halfway through the book I started the first exercise, and then a few more exercises. I had never known that I could control my thinking and that I could find a certain peace through meditation. I was so eager to learn that I wanted to race through all the exercises. Unfortunately, doing the exercises is not the only thing you have to do. There must also be some kind of spiritual growth, and that happens through the life experiences in daily life

I was in my mid twenties, had a full time job, was a part time criminal and had a drug addiction. I smoked at least nine joints a day, experimented with ecstasy and got into cocaine. Regardless of the lifestyle I had, I continued to focus on my work as a student.

After completing a number of exercises I joined Step 1 Magical Schooling Of The Soul Introspection.

Here I learned what Soul Mirror Work meant and started making the White and Black mirrors. I arrived at a point where I could not lie to myself and had to be a hundred percent honest. I read 'Be pitiless and very strict with yourself when it comes to your shortcomings, failings, habits, passions, urges and any other negative character traits.' This was certainly not an easy task. It was as if I was dissecting myself and I consisted of several personalities. I saw who I wanted to be and had to work very hard on myself. I did daily brushing, stretching exercises, auto-suggestion and impregnating food or drinks with wishes. Yes I did The Work. But because of a certain

PART I: INTROSPECTION

character trait I got distracted and finally in a deep hole. Due to the crime and the urge to make money quickly, I became involved with an organization that was involved in criminal activities. At the end of 2015 we were all arrested by the police and were sentenced to several months in prison.

Although the prison is not a nice place to be, this is the best thing that has happened to me in my life. Here I could think about my life. Here I was able to see what I had done wrong and what I needed to do to get a better life. In jail I didn't have my Magic diary with me but all my good and bad character traits were in my mind.

From there I decided to start working on myself. No more crime, no drugs, no greed, no impulsive behavior, but only seeing the white Mirror and becoming one with the divine. A few months later I was released and went to live with my girlfriend and her daughter.

We didn't have an easy start and I started to recognize more characteristics that I had to work on. Of course I had many good characteristics, but the negative ones always caused the problems. I was able to remove many negative traits altogether, but some of them are in a deep sleep. Those negative characteristics were still too strong to be completely out of my system. The daily exercises, meditation and books such as *The Universal Master Key* keep me strong. I also read many other books on the subject.

To this day, I have good control over my thoughts. By controlling my thought I have control of my feelings and emotion and by controlling my feelings and emotion I have control of my actions.

I think positively about life and people and in this way attract a lot of positivity. When I am somewhere I can load the space full of positivity and give people a good feeling. Children feel this and even animals. Now I work in hospitality and my employer sees my talents. I have a good salary, I am trained as a manager with many more career opportunities. I have been clean of drugs for three years, I am a good father to my stepdaughter and a good partner for my girlfriend. I know I have a long way to go as a student and will learn a lot. As Ben Parker said, 'With great power comes great responsibility'.

11. Soul Mirrors/Introspection/Triggers – Steve Vadney

As we work through creating our soul mirrors and start to analyze the what, how and why, that we do things or act a certain way, then we start to better understand how our mind works and how it is affected by influences, both internal and external; how external stimulants or triggers have an influential effect on our internal thoughts and our external actions. We reflect each night through introspection to assess the day, via our thoughts and actions, how we handled different situations and how we can improve, creating a more present minded state, as we go about each day.

As things happen, there is almost a sense of deja vu. Your intuition chimes with them and the memories of your previous experiences, as well as contemplation through introspection, trigger a thought or response that is based on these previous experiences. This gives you the opportunity to react more appropriately this time than previously. Now you start to recognize there is an issue and can become aware of it before it arises. A hurdle faced is triggers. These triggers are traps set along the way that can catch you off guard and can suggest to your subconscious that you do something. This can slow you down or even throw you completely off course. They may cause a change in emotional, mental, or physical actions. It could be instant or it could plant a seed which slowly grows into a bigger issue, but it starts a reaction/change.

Through introspection you start to notice these catalysts and become aware of them, which is one of the first steps in being able to regain control over them, or at least not to let them control you. Many triggers can create a negative reaction but you can also create your own triggers for your benefit. Triggers come in all forms and can have different effects on people. They can affect all of the senses; sound, smell, taste, touch, and sight. For example, the smell of foods can make you want to eat, even if you're not hungry. The smell of cigarettes make you want to smoke or turn you off from smoking. Seeing a billboard can put a thought of drinking or smoking or eating or spending money, into your head. Seeing other people going outside to smoke

PART I: INTROSPECTION

at work can cause you to want to do the same. Even the suggestion of another person saying, 'You want to go have a smoke'. The taste of coffee, or even just the thought of a coffee, can have the effect of wanting a cigarette. It can also be other things you do, habits you've developed that link together, such as coffee and cigarettes, pizza and beer, payday and a shopping spree. The association is also a trigger.

I worked with a recovering alcoholic at a pizza shop when I was younger. He couldn't discard the old, unused dough, because the yeast smell reminded him too much of alcohol. When I was younger I just thought it was an excuse not to have to do the task he was asked to do. As I got older I realized that the trigger of the smell had a dramatic effect on him and he would find himself back off the wagon.

Going to the movie theater, you are bombarded with smells, sights and sounds, all trying to get you to buy popcorn, soda and snacks. They trigger memories of past experiences, both good and bad, which create a response. Advertising is a perfect example. Its sole purpose is to influence. I like to refer to advertising and propaganda as black magick, probably because of the movie Wizards. It is produced to change your thoughts, opinions, or actions, and to get you to do what they want. You have billboards, radio, TV, internet, magazines and so on, all blasting you with subliminal messages to get you to do what they want you to do. The media is usually all about consumption and spending your money on whatever it is they have to sell.

The mind also has a funny way of allowing you to forget the negative experiences you've had in the past, or at least push them to a dark spot, so as not to traumatize you. So we forget and continue to repeat the same habit that we know is hindering us in some way. This also makes it more challenging to overcome. You may have drunk excessively the weekend before, then swore up and down that 'This is it – I'm never drinking again'. Then a week later, you had a rough day at work, it's hot out and someone says 'Hey, you want to go get a drink?' You find yourself back in the same situation, pushing the bad experience out of your thoughts and ending up in a similar situation again, wondering why you seem to forget so easily.

There are also the triggers that occur when you're even more in a subconscious state, for example when sleeping or inebriated. There are people who have disorders that, when awoken from sleep, may cause them to sleep walk, eat, talk and so on. Others may make comments and commit actions while intoxicated that they wouldn't normally do when awake and aware. These are more difficult changes, as you are in less control while they are going on. With intoxication, clearly with removing the intoxicant, you gain more control, but with sleep it is more difficult because you can't stop sleeping. However, these can still be dealt with and ultimately controlled.

Once you see what the cause or trigger is, you can start to form a plan to correct it. You can start to control it, either ignoring it or facing it head on. Bardon gives you the steps to create change in yourself. The techniques of the 'six-pronged attack' are very good in assisting you in making these improvements. You can make yourself aware of them, so as they arise you can have a plan. Better yet, even try to prevent them before they occur. You can also create counter-triggers or positive triggers. Make yourself aware of how you react when a certain trigger is present and change how you react to it. There are items that can be used to help create a positive change or build a positive habit, such as jewelry – pins, bracelets, stones, gratitude rock or notes; for example sticky notes, motivational calendars, phrases written and placed in specific places, or written on the mirror, even paper or a note card you carry in your pocket – a prayer card is one example. Even situations such as driving home from work or touching a door knob are very mundane things and can all be used to create a trigger.

Gratitude. It's good to have something to remind you to be thankful for in life. I feel that helps with continuing a positive flow. Two things I've done in the past, at the recommendation of a friend, were to keep a gratitude rock in my pocket and to create a gratitude list. The following are some examples, but the possibilities are endless. The gratitude list isn't necessarily a trigger, at least at first, but it can be as you spend more time adding to it – it will gain more significance and build a memory. It can help you think about positive influences in your life, which does have a positive effect. At first it is very easy to think about things you're thankful for, being alive, having discovered hermetics or your spiritual path, or your family and people in your life. Add one new item to the list each day and as the days go on, you may have to dig deeper to see what else you're thankful for. Originally when it was suggested I do this, I wasn't told how long to do it for. I continued for over 100 days, eventually being told it was only necessary to do twenty one days, as that is

PART I: INTROSPECTION

the said time needed to create a new habit. It can and will have a strong impact on how you look at things. The late Dr. Wayne Dyer said 'If you change the way you look at things, the things you look at will change'. You start to be thankful for everything and start to appreciate things that you took for granted, for example, the sky, nature and colors. Even the people in your life who you aren't a big fan of, because even they have an impact on you and your life, even if it is just a reminder of how not to act. But you learn to appreciate it all and start to get a glimpse into some of the lessons and purpose of these interactions. The gratitude rock however is more direct. The idea is that every time you put your hand in your pocket and touch it, it reminds you to be grateful and to think about something you're grateful for. It has a positive uplifting effect. It is just a rock, a random stone that someone picked up off the ground. Sure it could be charged with positive attributes to increase the effects, but it isn't necessary, because it is a physical trigger. It does work best if given to someone and explained in the way of it being a gratitude rock and that it has the ability to remind you to be grateful. That will associate this rock with gratefulness. That is all you need, the association, for it will work. You can use physical items such as notes or jewelry, or you can use non-physical triggers such as meditation, introspection and breathing. You can use these things to remind you to go to bed and get enough sleep, to relax, not to be angry, to exercise, to breathe or even to remember to smile throughout the day. You can even take a negative trigger and try to change its association to a positive trigger, such as when you recognize the urge to smoke, try to use that as an opportunity to focus on breathing or meditation, or other health-related things that are the opposite of what smoking is.

By recognizing the triggers, what they are, how they influence us and learning how to overcome them, change them, or combat them with positive triggers, we can regain control and help in our advancement with the balance of our soul. Staying busy is also a good thing to do. Idle time can be a trigger that leads to other negative traits. The less idle time you have and the more focused you are on the task in hand, the less influence the subliminal messages and triggers will have. Like misery, negative traits enjoy company. So the sooner you start to chip away at them, the easier it will become. By eliminating one, you start to chip away at triggers that influence another. It is all interwoven.

PART I: INTROSPECTION

12. Goal Setting and Introspection – Aaron Wolfe

It can be said that Introspection, especially as Bardon introduces it, is the praxis by which you are able to answer the age-old question: who am I? The answer to this question, in the form of the Soul Mirrors, is the foundation of the entire Bardonian system of Magic and Hermetic Philosophy. This also lays the foundation for a second question, one rarely considered with as much depth as the first: who do I want to be? Or perhaps more aptly, who do I have the potential to be? This question is as important as the first, and it needs to be answered as concretely as the first question does. One of the best methods of doing this is with the practice of goal setting, for everyone needs dreams and purpose in their life to sustain them, and the art of goal setting is an excellent way to pursue that end. Giants of the inspirational speaking world like Jim Rohn and Zig Ziglar have long since taught the art of goal setting in depth, but here we can consider its application to Bardon's praxis. The art of goal setting for soul mirror work can be broken into the three main steps: developing and setting goals, reverse engineering those goals to determine how to achieve them, and how goals can lay a map towards magical equipoise.

There are three fundamental types of goals. Financial goals are those which define your career and financial aspirations, including what promotions you want, what income you want, what savings you want, and so on. All goals regarding money, career, and retirement go on this list of goals. Material goals are the things you want in life, including what kind of house you want, what kind of car, what kind of computer, and so on. Do not disregard this because you deem yourself spiritual, above materialism, or any other such nonsense. If you are reading this, even if you are sufficiently detached from worldly affairs, you are a material being living in a society that requires financial and material participation. Control this, or it will control you. Personal Development goals are those which define how you want to grow as a person in life, including what languages you want to learn, what skills you want to acquire, and how you want to interact with the world.

The goal of being a Magician is, of course, a Personal Development goal just as Soul Mirror praxis is Personal Development praxis. These three types of goals can be broken up further into timed goals: goals that you want to achieve in the next ten years, goals you want to achieve in five years, three years, one year, six months, and you can even set weekly and daily goals. After all, it is the daily commitments that define the decade.

In creating goals, it is useful to make them all S.M.A.R.T. goals. Specific, Measurable, Attainable, Realistic, and Timed. Specific goals are important because ambiguity serves little good, particularly in the work of self-knowledge. Instead of saying something like 'I want to be rich,' specify clearly something like 'I want to make a million dollars per year' or 'I want a net worth over one million dollars.' The generality 'rich' is too relative and ambiguous, but specific goals can be broken up and understood. Measurable also plays into this. 'Rich' is not a measurable goal, but a million dollars per year, or a million-dollar net worth, are measurable. As for Attainable and Realistic, that has to be determined by breaking them into smaller goals and also considering Time. Will you make a million dollars per year this particular year? Maybe not, but if you build a business and work hard for ten years or more, it is possible eventually to make a million dollars per year or have a net worth over a million dollars. The ten year to daily goal scale mentioned previously is also part of timing your goals. This makes S.M.A.R.T. goals, and every other goal must be approached in this way. As a more specific example, 'I want to be a Magician' is too general, but 'I want to complete Step 10 of Initiation into Hermetics' is a S.M.A.R.T. goal that leads to that same end.

Once you have built your three lists of S.M.A.R.T. goals, break them down into smaller steps of achievement to get more clarity on how exactly you might achieve them. 'I want to complete Step 10 of Initiation into Hermetics,' for example, is a daunting challenge by itself – but Bardon already has this goal broken into much smaller steps that can be tackled one at a time until you reach that end goal. Every other goal must be approached in this same manner. What steps do you need to complete to make a million dollars? What steps do you need to complete to become fluent in a language you want to learn? Whatever your goals are, break them down into smaller, more digestible steps. This can be daunting to do on all of your life goals, so

PART I: INTROSPECTION

pick three to six big things to focus on first. You can repeat this periodically as you achieve your goals.

At this point, it is possible to achieve a deeper layer of introspection in the present Soul Mirrors. Take your three to six big goals, broken into steps, and compare them to qualities in your Soul Mirror. What in your White Mirror already exists that is helping you build the future you want? Better yet, what personality traits and habits are required for your goal that need to be acquired? Examine your vices, too: what traits and habits in your life are preventing you from achieving your goal? Examine this not just by looking at the vices you've already listed, but specifically by examining your habits in relation to what it takes to achieve your goals, so that you may uncover vices you had previously missed. This reverse-engineering of your goals will not only deepen introspection and soul mirror work, but also help you understand better exactly how to succeed in achieving your life goals.

One more step can be taken after this to better understand the journey to magical equipoise. It is important to understand that goals change as humans grow and change. This, in part, is a reflection of our inner elemental balance, and as such all of the previous work on developing S.M.A.R.T. goals can be used as a guide to elemental equipoise. For example, if your biggest goals are financial, you might find many of these to be of Earth in their root, and perhaps some of Fire. Intellectual goals, such as learning another language, may often be more of Air. Each goal and each aspect of your goals can be examined for elemental alignment like this, to serve as a guide toward equipoise, as a sort of preliminary to the more advanced work in Step 8: using concentration disturbances as a guide to equipoise. This isn't something that should be jumped into, but once the other goal setting and introspection praxis is done, this can be done to further deepen and develop the work.

Through the work of goal setting to deepen contemporary introspection, you acquire the ability to answer the question: *who do I have the potential to be?* And, by answering this question to fulfilment, you ultimately answer the deeper question of gnosis: *who am I?* These questions create a feedback loop. As you understand your goals, and what it takes to achieve them, you begin to understand yourself on a deeper level. This, like soul mirror work and the attainment and maintenance of equipoise, is a lifelong praxis that has much potential.

Part II: Understanding Magical Equilibrium

PART II: UNDERSTANDING MAGICAL EQUILIBRIUM

1. The Multidimensional Equilibrium Process - Muhammad Husain Ali Baig.

In order to understand magical equilibrium, I'd like for you to think of the number 7. Now let's break 7 up into 3 and 4. 3 represents your spirit (mental body), soul (astral body), and physical body. 4 represents the 4 elements of mind, body, soul (fire, water, earth, air).

In order to attain equilibrium you need to balance the 4 elements in each of your 3 bodies.

For attaining elemental equilibrium in your mental body, you must learn to split your awareness onto your will (fire), intelligence (air), feelings (water), and consciousness (earth), all at the same time. This could be called Quadra concentration, or the four-pole magnet. A skill /muscle that every true magician must build. With practice, your mental body will always operate with a balanced amount of the 4 elements; thereby enhancing the power of your magical work greatly.

We live in a world where most people's mental bodies are elementally imbalanced; i.e. some folks are heavily aware of their feelings and are often dominated by them, yet they have little to no awareness of their will. Others are highly intelligent, and are well versed in the world of intellect, but they have no understanding of feelings and their intuitive wisdom. You get the idea. Mastering one element in the mental body won't cut it. You need balance.

Attaining elemental balance in the astral body is a bit more tricky. To begin effectively working on elemental balance of your astral body, you must have achieved an at least somewhat balanced mental body.

In order to perceive the astral realm and your astral body, use your feelings and vacant awareness. Feel for the 'enemies' around you and within your aura; this is the astral. Immediately you'll notice knots, twists and turns, energy spikes, blockages, etc. Welcome to the astral. This is where most of the tough work happens. Use your will, to undo the knots and blockages in your astral body. You'll find many of the astral blocks are related/connected to mental limitations or beliefs you held. As you are working on refining and cleaning the energies of your astral body, you'll begin to feel how the various energies of the astral are different from one another; this will lead you to being able to differentiate between the 4 elements in the astral (i.e. you'll feel the difference between expansive, jittery, fire energy and dense, slow, earth energy).

As you get better with your work in the astral, you'll find yourself switching from clearing random limiting energy blocks, to creating and structuring energetic channels for positive character trait building (for building an elementally balanced astral body). Building an elementally balanced astral body involves literally building tangible forms of energy using breath. However one must be careful to connect with their deepest intuition during this work in order to ensure the work is done properly; trust intuition over belief systems you may have picked up over a lifetime of reading, analyzing, and theorizing.

Finally you must attain elemental balance within your physical body. This involves balance in both your physical body as well as the life of your individual self in this world and society. To attain balance in this worldly life you must remember the elemental correspondences. Fire represents your power and drive in life and it's sought after goals. Air is the intellectual side of life; what you read, your philosophy, your way of using your intelligence, etc. Water represents the feeling and love part of life; family, friends, intimacy, enjoyment, fun, adventure, action, inspiration, etc. Earth represents your deepest desires and purposes; what you create in this world.

When trying to understand how to balance worldly life, I like to split worldly life into finances, (air) relationships (water), spirituality/mental mastery (fire), and physical bodily health (earth). You must master each one of these four things in your worldly life as a human. This seemingly 'regular' part of life is still very important for every magician to master in order to attain true magical equilibrium.

You have to ensure that the life you live in this physical world is balanced and strong. A magician with an imbalanced worldly life only limits their own power and magical ability.

Aside from bringing balance to your worldly life, you must also bring elemental balance literally to your physical body. This means that you work with your organs, blood, nerves, bones, muscles, glands, etc. to bring elemental balance. This can be done with intention, will, breath, and movement. Remember that just as you literally rebuilt your astral body for elemental balance, so will you do the same with your physical body.

PART II: UNDERSTANDING MAGICAL EQUILIBRIUM

All of this 4-fold balancing work in your 3 bodies is obviously a long process. This is work that you must must do seriously and with dedication. It is very serious and mandatory work, as your soul evolution depends on you attaining equilibrium.

Important Tips:

1. Remember the importance of breath in maneuvering the energies of the astral and other bodies.
2. Don't forget about the fifth element. Akasa. Connect with it via surrender to begin it's work.
3. Work on self realization, godhead connection, and understanding the universal laws (quabbalistic keys).

2. The Magical Balance – Angel of God

The magical balance is nothing more than common sense. Nothing more than that – common sense that in everyday attitudes has goodness and common sense. Indeed the heart must speak and act, but with common sense. If God gave us brains, there is no shadow of a doubt we should use it, and not refrain from doing so out of fear of wearing it out.

The balance takes place mainly in the day-to-day life with those close to us – above all with the family. These do need more care and common sense than the others. If God gave one such a family, surely it was to get out of it some result, not just for hateful and hurtful fights.

The elements that the universe presents to you as fire, water, air and earth are nothing more than representations of teachings – cosmic virtues that you once understood better – but at the moment it is enough to know that the elements are correlations of the people and situations around you. If for example you have a lot of fire element, the universe will inevitably place someone of water element around you, to contrast with you and to teach you the characteristic of water and its analogous virtues. There are no co-incidences – only action and reaction.

But you must be asking yourself 'Why should a person who is my opposite be close to me and often live with me?' The answer is simple, my brother – to help each other in your cosmic evolution. The different are different only up to a certain point. Then they complement each other and help each other. One pushes the other, thus making great progress; we well know how painful and difficult this trial can be, but if overcome … Great and immense pleasure you will have when you arrive in the happy worlds.

The elements are nothing more than analogies for situations that you do not understand, but know that all things have a reason for being. Nothing happens by chance. The opposite elements have the mission of 'annulling' themselves, that is, if you understand. Do not think that water is so far from fire, nor fire is so far from water. On the contrary the two are very similar in ways that only a great initiate would understand, but know when different people coexist it is always for greater reasons that they themselves can understand.

PART II: UNDERSTANDING MAGICAL EQUILIBRIUM

Balance is not in the false posture of a sage or even the false posture of a hermit. Balance is in living each day thinking that this may be the last, as in fact for many it is – not in exaggerations of voluptuousness, gluttony and other exaggerations, but in the good sense that much is bad, and little is little. The balance is not only in daily choices, but is in walking, in eating without biting the tongue, in breathing without exaggeration. But I say the main point of balance that Bardon secretly asks us, is in the treatment of those around us. Perhaps it seems lame, but it is not. The elements manifest themselves strongly in those around us.

For example, do you want to progress in the practice of heating or cooling the body? This is very simple, as long as the Initiate has in mind that the beings around us have much to teach us. The fire, for example, is endowed with great courage and tenor; its brilliance drives away the darkness of ignorance and inspires the other three elements with its bravery. But at the same time anger can ignite in the heart of the adept or even the layman and real tragedies can occur.

So where's the balance? Is it in the lack of water to balance the fire element, or is it the lack of understanding of this magnificent element that causes such tragedies? Dear reader, for this point, whatever your answer is, both in the lack and in the deeper and more profound understanding of the element in question, you will be right.

A faulty knowledge of one's own nature is what causes the most terrible tragedies on the planes that are confined to the living.

Where are the four elements? What are the four elements? What is ether? What is life? Where am I, where am I going? What exists on the other side? Why was I born here? Why all of this? Until when?

Dear Initiate, magicians are not born from lies, but from the truth. It is not with lies that you will reach maximum power. Stop deceiving yourself thinking that only with breaths and absorption of elements will you have power.

Power is born of will and will is born of will! But whose will? The 'I' or the ego?

Do you really think that the ego can do anything with your life? Who do you think put you in the situation you are in? For some, the situation may be more comfortable, or even pleasant. But do not deceive yourselves. Time passes and at some point the account of the sordid and harmful past of some will come. just like the pearls sown hard with pain and tears.

Life is more than 'having'. Life is a treasure, which some insist on spending on things that lead to nothing. Or do you think it's just the one hundred years here on earth and it's over?

To avoid tears and much remorse, start now to practice the essence of the Gospels, the essence of Bardon's teachings. Do you really think courage is in the fire? For do you know that it is just the opposite, that fire is in courage, not the opposite, and do you know where the greatest of all courage is? Look with eyes of humility and supreme reverence to the cross that was sanctified with the blood of Christ Himself, who gave the maximum example.

The balance is not in lies, but in truth, and the only truth that you can really have and make the most of is in the simple gestures of kindness and understanding that you have with your brothers and sisters and perhaps after much practice and swallowing thorns, perhaps then you will start to spit roses and then and only then will you know the true power.

PART II: UNDERSTANDING MAGICAL EQUILIBRIUM

3. The Four Pillars of the Temple – Crystalf Maibach

As you are probably aware, Franz Bardon in his first book *Initiation into Hermetics* (IIH), which is about the becoming of the Magician, the author mentions in Step 3 the well-known formulas of 'To know, to dare, to will, to be silent' (in German: Wissen, Wagen, Wollen, Schweigen). While that formula is cited quite often, in many conversations with aspiring students I feel that these precepts are not fully grasped, but instead looked upon as quite superficial in comparison with the practical exercises. Sadly, nonetheless many students struggle with those; maybe even because they ignore the context too much. As these formulas are indeed pillars to work upon, I decided to write my following article about them to help students to understand them fully and also to benefit from them, as those are cornerstones of the hermetic personality. In the following pages I will try to bring up some topics that are specifically found in the circles of Bardon practitioners and bring them into a wider, initiatory context.

***

To Know (WISSEN):

While this is the first of the four pillars, it is in my observation the one that is most likely to be ignored by practitioners – the more the people love to practice, the more they seem to ignore this pillar. But it is the foundation, the Earth Element of the four Pillars, not the Air, which might be the first thought, as will become obvious later. There seem to be two kinds of people: those who despise Bardon and read whole libraries of other things and those who love him and then tend to point out, that 'there is only one book you need', and that is, of course IIH. Obviously both extremes are quite lacking.

While I come back to the first category of people later, let's stay for a moment with the second type. I can well understand them, as Bardon's books are very enchanting in their magical atmosphere, so for some time I had those ideas too. Luckily I never stuck to them. One of the direst dangers in occultism is the danger of 'Guru-ism': to only concentrate on one author or one teacher, who is considered superior to all the others. That is the reason why I don't like being dubbed a 'Bardonist', even though I am probably known best as that. But I am not, since my approach is not about the man Franz Bardon, but about the systematic he creates in his works, about the way he categorizes the exercises, which by themselves can be found in many a German occult book, for example by Karl Spiesberger.

To make the difference between author and work is very important. Thus when a student claims that they need only one book, which is IIH, the first part of the Formula – To Know – is casually ignored. Despite some prejudices by certain occultists, Bardon's work is not about making hermetic students into devout Bardonists, but to help the student to become self-conscious Magicians. And to reach this lofty goal, he makes absolutely clear that it is necessary to obtain occult knowledge.

This can most easily be obtained by reading good books. 'Good books' in this case of course doesn't mean just the standard fare of 'How to do a LBPR!', but instead books that make the student understand why they are doing what they are doing. That's especially hard for the pure anglophone speaker as most of the books that Bardon used are only available in Czech and especially German. Nonetheless, it's possible and important to study and understand Yoga, Asana, Dharana, Rosicrucianism, Alchemy, Astrology, Ritual Magic, Aleister Crowley, Kabbalah and so on. Only a most extensive study will sufficiently support the student of Hermeticsm to truly understand the PATH they are walking on.

But beware: of course that shall not mean that theoretical knowledge is the sole purpose of initiation. Instead this is only recommended to bring further understanding to those who claim their quite religious 'Only One Book With One Truth' mentality. Bardons books are NOT heaven sent to bring The One Truth, but instead a system carefully constructed to spare the student the time to bring the million different exercises available into a logical order. Thus, practice is the core of initiation, which will be further examined in the 'To Dare' section, but the practice is to be understood and bolstered by the theoretical knowledge of Hermetics.

Even in modern fantasy literature the Magician is known to be very knowledgeable, a transcendent scientist (German: Geheimwissenschaftler) even, who deeply understands not only himself – that's just the foundation, achieved in Steps 1 and 2 – but is deeply engaged in the occult laws of

PART II: UNDERSTANDING MAGICAL EQUILIBRIUM

reality, capable of understanding fate and sending heroes to quests, make potions, take on natural invisible beings and so on. And no less is the claim that Bardon makes in his books and also tried to live by.

If you really want to cling to one book giving you the truth, it would be better to buy yourself a Bible or a Quran, go into the desert for ten years and hope for the best.

To Dare (WAGEN):

This pillar is in many ways the opposite of the first one – courage not only to read, but to act as well. It's airy as it involves a lot of thinking. This is the one pillar which the most theoretical occultists, so-called Armchair Magicians, and especially conspiracy theorists tend to ignore. Only by acting, by practical work can true change be achieved, and thus true initiation. To only read things and think about them gives knowledge, but not wisdom and for sure not power. To stress the fantasy image of the magician, a pure theorist would never become a magician. They would become a pure scientist maybe or a book worm, but as we can see in the present state of the world, many scientists, while well-read, lack wisdom, as their works are traded freely, without the ethical barriers found in occultism.

A true magician consists of knowledge and wisdom – and other abilities we talk about in the next two sections. Wisdom and strength, maturity and change are made by acting; by striving forward, forward into regions the non-initiated might not dare to walk. But the students of hermetics, eager to become magicians, dare to walk there. They start to meditate, confront themselves with their worst characteristics, their weaknesses and especially their mistakes. They start to confront themselves with the things in their surroundings they feared so far. They take up courage to look, where they didn't dare to look before, to act upon what they feared to do before. They start to stand up for those in need, regarding how they can help them. For example, a well-known German magician, Gregor A. Gregorius, even threw himself before a driving car to rescue a little bug on the street and was nearly badly injured.

But of course, there's a downside to this: to act also means to fail; it means inevitably to suffer. But as Bardon loves to point out: life isn't a fairground. And even suffering has purpose: to learn. To suffer means to grow. Only by suffering themselves the students learn what it means for other human and animal and plant beings to suffer as well. And only this deep empathic understanding leads to true wisdom. The best advice is to be aware of the gain and the potential suffering that can be expected by following certain behaviors of your fellow humans.

Human suffering cannot ultimately be ended by the Magician, but the Magician is capable of helping those who come to him, to make deep inner peace with their suffering – and help themselves. And this is only possible if the Magician has dared to confront what hurts him and make peace with it. Daring to confront Saturn, the Keeper of the Threshold and walk though his dark portal, just to see him smile in a light blue Jovian light. But many aspiring magicians fail initiation and stay on the early steps, because they lack the courage to truly dare to walk the Path, since they don't want to fight against the darkness in themselves, but rather stay in their comfort zone of food, money, sex and even the things that gives them pain, but at least they think they know of. In fact they fear to draw away the curtain, even when deep down in themselves they feel that there is so much more to be gained by delving into their own darkness. That's why we need the Will – it's the balance between Knowledge and Courage, which builds a solid foundation for the practice of Initiation and ultimately magic, the ability to change even reality.

To Will (WOLLEN):

In modern occultism the meaning of Will has developed a very specific meaning, mostly by the work of Aleister Crowley. And even while Bardon was by no means a Thelemite in the actual meaning of that word, he was indeed influenced by Crowley's ideas about Will and Love, which we can find in several stages of IIH.

In hermetic meaning, the Will is very fiery – the strength to strive forward. It gives foundation to Daring, even makes daring and courage possible. Thus as the fiery part in us, the Element of fire even resembles the divine part or spark in all of us, which leads our Path and can even lead to godhead. Fire is the first of the Elements, the first manifestation moving out of the unmanifested. And thus we need it to manifest our inner divinity. Simply put, it's not enough just to want initiation, we need to Will it. We as human beings want a lot of things, mostly of a carnal nature – food, money, respect, sex – even fame or independence belongs to this category.

PART II: UNDERSTANDING MAGICAL EQUILIBRIUM

The goals of this wanting change quite often – as soon as a certain wanting is fulfilled we turn to the next one. That's the simple reason why most humans are never really happy, since they always lack something. That is of course the reason for human development on a material plane, but obviously from the experience of ages, it is not enough for Initiation. Initiation is too long-winded, too ephemeral to give satisfaction to the pure wanting of body or unmanifested need.

A lot of students start the exercises and have some expectations of what they think initiation is about and then don't gain immediate satisfaction and promptly become bored, or the feeling that they do something wrong and quit again. But in truth they simply have not yet developed the Will to do the exercises just for doing them. They want something of a carnal nature out of Initiation, but the only reason for initiation is initiation, just for growing, just for being the magician, not for doing something with the magic. Or in Step 1 just for observing their thoughts. That's one of the reasons why the Will is considered divine, as it stands above the need for immediate satisfaction. It's a deep inner longing which doesn't need results, just acting.

For those who now think all is lost, don't worry; no one is simply born with the Awareness of this Will, it is something that needs to be realized by the student. Even the best magicians probably started out with obscure goals in their heads. But Initiation helps with that, if undertaken properly – that's why Thought Observation is the first and MOST important exercise in IIH for the beginner. It helps the student, when undertaken thoroughly, to understand themselves better, to realize where their true Will really lies, as they realize the insubstantiality of their desires.

Thus to Will is not to desire or to wish – it's something more elemental. The Will defines you in your most inner being. Desire always leads to compulsions and the need for carnal satisfaction. The Will leads you to your own personal Path. And in the case of a magician to the Awakening – the development of mystical-magical personality and maturity, but only if the student finds their Will in walking that Path. And that is the true reason why the mysteries always protect themselves – the Path is so long and even sometimes dull or hard, that only those who REALLY want to walk the Path of magical heights reach the mountain top. The rest remains behind... *Multi Convocat, Pauci Electi!*

To be silent (SCHWEIGEN):

Bardon characterizes this virtue mainly as 'not bragging', which is indeed true, but probably also very seldom to be used at all in the life of the average student. With whom do you brag about your magic? Mostly other Magicians. For most students it's not the case too often to meet other magicians in person, just in the internet. In our day and age the pillar of being silent is mostly important considering the interaction with our friends and family – and the internet.

The student should not talk about his Path with his friends and family for two reasons – first, so as not to become unmotivated. When you tell your family you're working on becoming a Magician and they break into laughs, well, that can be quite unmotivating. Even while that might be a little bit too extreme an example, the point is that the doubt, mild laughing, confusion of others can hinder the student on their way quite significantly – especially at the beginning. Many still need the support of others to judge about right and wrong – and that trait needs to be erased by the self-conscious peace of the strong person, sure of their ways. Thus when the student has reached a certain stage of maturity and experience and has performed several magical feats themselves and therefore doesn't need belief or self-assurance, but KNOWS and is strong in their will – a stage of magical development comparable to the beginning of Step 9 – then it becomes easier to talk about his achievements with the uninitiated without the danger of doubt coming into his mind.

The same applies to posting on Facebook or other social media. Of course, everybody can post on social media and get a lot of support, but that's simply not the assurance a Magician needs, as it won't help the slightest in magical work. Just the opposite – it can lead the beginner to false illusions about his own stage of development. So I do recommend not talking or writing about your inner experiences before you have reached the aforementioned stage of maturity.

But beware – no matter how high you are in your development, to remain silent will always be one of the core pillars of initiation. Just because the doubt of others cannot shake the student as easily as on the early stages of the Path, it doesn't mean they shall talk openly about their experiences. In fact something should in every situation always stay secret.

PART II: UNDERSTANDING MAGICAL EQUILIBRIUM

The second reason to remain silent is to 'get pressure on the cooking pot'. When after each exercise or magical experiment the student runs around and tells everybody, no matter whether friends, family or even other magicians about the results of their work, it loses significance. That might feel good when the work was a failure, because lost significance of failure might lead to less worrying, but that is quite self-delusionary – and nonetheless it becomes less special, more so every day, more grey, more boring. And even worse in the case of successes – then all the student gets is the short-lived praise of others. And if they still need that – what does it tell about their self-consciousness? Of course it's understandable when a student after a successful evocation wants to tell everybody about the manifested Being, but then the bragging starts – or the doubt of others.

This most intimate and special success, the result of years of training becomes something to be discussed, to be doubted, to be no more special than the news on television. Do you want that? I guess not. Of course, as well as before, even here nothing stops the magician later from writing about some parts of their experiences, to discuss it with students or teach about it. Magic is not something that has to be kept in the Magician's mind forever, or no spellbook would ever have been written but always after the experience itself has been deeply rooted in the spirit and soul of the Magician. When it has become part of them as much as walking, then the time has come to talk or teach about it, but not earlier. And especially not directly following the experience itself. For the student: silence. For the Master: teaching, without sharing the intimate details of the work. That is what silence can lead to.

***

To have the Will to be patient, to dare to trust yourself, as you know you're taking strength from silence will lead YOU to further Ascension.
Good Luck!

4. ON MAGICAL EQUILIBRIUM – WILLIAM R. MISTELE

Novice: Now then Sir, I wish to inquire regarding magical equilibrium.

Older Novice: Very well. What exactly did you have in mind?

Novice: Well, I am supposed to balance the four elements in my soul making the weak stronger and the negative positive. Got any tips on doing that?

Older Novice: I thought Franz Bardon's *Initiation into Hemetics* was perfectly clear on how to do this. Just follow the directions. Like a can of Campbell's soup, follow the directions and you get cooked soup.

Novice: Yes, I am sure there is a 'one size fits all' approach to magical training. I am equally certain that somewhere on the planet earth there is a Bardon student who says to himself, 'Ah. That was a lot of work. But now I have attained a magical equilibrium that is convincing and stable. Time to move on to chapter III.

'The problem is, that there is a cultural and archetypal abyss between chapter II and chapter III. In chapter III of *Initiation into Hermetics* Bardon introduces us to creating and dissolving the fire element in our soul exactly as a baby salamander in training might learn to master fire.

'See how swiftly we have moved from chapters I and II in attaining a balance of the four elements in our soul as we observe our present personality as it functions within society and then we move on right away to working with the four elements as they exist in nature and in the greater universe.

'And not only that. Sometimes growing up we have already been exposed to problems as they arise from archetypal levels of the collective and global subconscious. It is all nice and good to say, "You need to bring into balance in a positive and constructive way the elements of earth, air, fire, and water in your soul."

'But the hard, cold fact is that Homo sapiens has never been in balance in the last two hundred thousand years of his existence. You are asking an individual to do what has never been accomplished before. Our entire culture

PART II: UNDERSTANDING MAGICAL EQUILIBRIUM

and civilization is skewed to deceive and deny us from undertaking such a task.'

Older Novice: Okay. I see where you are going with this. Let's start slowly. I am sure you have heard all of his before. Let's take fire then. It represents will and power. You know, some people exude physical power. You can feel a force in their presence like a martial arts master or a ghetto street fighter. Their adrenal glands are ready to unleash this individual's energy in a concentrated manner.

Then there is astral fire. This gives an electrifying enthusiasm, dynamic conviction and confidence, and charisma, like excitement and passionate desire, are ever driving the individual forward.

After all, for men who make it through puberty, they find something worth doing that is right for them and that is totally captivating. Fail in this task and you live your life in the shadows of other men's accomplishments.

In effect, fire on the astral plane is the emotional energy unleashed that takes hold of the world and changes it. You can have a dream, ideals, resolution, and commitments. This astral fire is the force that lights up that dream, lays hold of that ideal, empowers your resolution, and focuses your energy to fulfil your commitments.

Similarly, fire on the mental plane is the exact power you need to accomplish your plans in life. You can draw up a brilliant plan of action. Lay out all the steps you need to follow through in getting the results you want. But without the sheer power of will that keeps you focused, wards off all distractions, and laser-like zeros in on what you need to do each day, your plans will not come to be.

And then there is akashic fire. Sometimes you must be united to the divine to bring about changes in the world. Nothing else will do. It is like having the authority, the command, orders handed down, if you are to overcome seemingly impossible obstacles.

Then again, as you insist, most people are limited by their childhood experience and development as to how they approach fire, will, and power, though some overcome all obstacles. If you grow up in a feudal, autocratic society, a dictatorship, or a democracy, you are going to have a different understanding of what power is and the part you can play in society.

If your father was a general or a CEO who runs a global corporation, you have a different sense of command, personal initiative, self-direction, and resolve than if your father was a teacher or union steward. It is quite difficult to identify with other kinds of power if your family background is all about tradition and honor versus a family of inventors, innovators, and entrepreneurs.

Our modern society enables the quick acquisition of power in many different forms. You may have a high school coach who was a captain in the marines. He will drill you and demand you perform at your highest level. Something of his self-control and will he will transfer to you through his tone of voice, body language, his training procedures, and his expectations.

You may have had a work situation where the supervisor or CEO contained a great deal of power. His managerial style was demanding and he was ever watchful, again, asking those under him to perform at their highest levels. When an alpha male is present who is dynamic, positive, successful, and purpose driven, something of that leadership style rubs off on you.

You can sit and think positive thoughts about focusing your will all you want. But it is never going to be the same as actually having lived through situations where a great deal of power is in play every day. And nothing is quite the same as sitting at a dinner table and having someone explain to you 'Here is how I turned that enemy into a friend.' 'Here is how I warded off the union strike.' 'Here is how I took command of a corrupt organization.' 'Here is how we convinced the jury that the federal government was wrong.' 'Here is how I dealt with my superior officers when they were arrogant and mistaken.' 'Here is how I dealt with the police when they thought they were going to arrest me.' 'Here is what I said to Henry Ford when he questioned my ability.' And so on.

You want power; at some point you will need direct experience with how human beings in difficult situations manage to command and direct power successfully in overcoming great opposition. Now you know what power is. And from your experience you can successfully compare and contrast positive and negative uses of power. And you can then generalize to some extent about applications of power in completely different situations.

Novice: So martial art training, business supersizing and managerial positions, and leadership positions with groups of people expose an individual to the force of astral fiery energy?

Older Novice: That is right. Nothing like experience.

PART II: UNDERSTANDING MAGICAL EQUILIBRIUM

Novice: So what about the weak and negative sides of fire?

Older Novice: Right. Like fire, if you are exposed to an abuse of power, it can burn you. Some people will identify with their perpetrators because they see how effective the abusive individual is in getting what he wants. That external fire gets inside of you and possesses you, imprinting its selfish desires on you.

On the other hand, if you are burnt by fire/will, you may become passive as a result and shy away from using power yourself because you do not want to become like those negative examples. That negative fire is in you but you do everything you can to keep it in check.

It took an outsider and a professional team of investigative reporters to begin to expose the hundreds of thousands of children who were abused by priests and brothers in the Catholic Church. Yet almost none of those abused children found the power in themselves to demand that the Church change. The massive institution of the Catholic Church, like other rooted traditions, drains the will of those who would oppose them. And even in an advanced, democratic society change can be slow. It often takes between six and fifty years to change wrongs being committed by corporations or government.

Power is often held by institutions whose only real commitment is to preserving themselves. Will and power are not abstract things. They are embedded in every aspect of society.

When power is abused for decades, for generations, or for hundreds of years or millennia, it is going to take a great deal of applied force and intelligence to bring about change. And then the reformers, when they arise, often make things worse by failing to address the root cause of the abuses of power. They become like to, or worse than, those they are attempting to reform.

Novice: You talk like the I-Ching. You can have a superior man of noble will but there are times when he should lay low because the external world will destroy him if he tries to do the right thing. But if conditions are right, then there is a time to put forth all your might to seize the opportunity that presents itself.

Older Novice: Exactly. So a great deal can in fact be said for trying to improve oneself before becoming involved in the external world. And at the same time, without experience in the external world, a great deal of one's training is worthless because there is nothing to test it against. Meditation and focusing your thoughts provides very little feedback regarding the quality and effectiveness of developing power and will.

Novice: So if one gets angry?

Older Novice: Anger results from failure to focus on our priorities and purposes. Study anger management so you don't have to reinvent the wheel. And of course discover what triggers your own anger by reviewing past situations where you have observable patterns in the way and in the situations in which you get angry.

There is personal anger. There is collective anger. There is righteous anger. Sometimes something needs to be destroyed. Someone must come forward to protect the needy, the innocent, and the vulnerable. Otherwise, injustice prevails.

Novice: What about bitterness, resentment, whining, and complaining?

Older Novice: You know, maybe it is just me. But I have taken a kind of vow never to whine or complain and that extends to feeling bitter and resentful. Life is too short. And there is so much wonder and beauty surrounding me. Why would I throw poison into a well?

Novice: What about manipulation, deception, lies, and controlling others?

Older Novice: Fire needs fuel to burn – that is its greatest weakness – and it also emits light. A low grade fire gives off lots of smoke, waste, and pollution. A purer fire has little or no smoke and it burns hotter. When you have experience, you accomplish the most with the least effort.

So if you consider the signs of Aries, Leo, and Sagittarius, the Aries individual often acts in a straightforward and bold manner. But he leaves a mess for others to clean up because he is not taking into consideration how his bold actions affect others.

The Leo draws people together to form a community. But to offer so much affection and leadership to others the Leo will often demand loyalty

PART II: UNDERSTANDING MAGICAL EQUILIBRIUM

and demand that others give him a lot of attention. Someone has to be at the center. A mature Leo, however, is free of ego so he assists others to shine.

The Sagittarian is on a quest, seeking justice, or pursuing an ideal. But his will is focused with such enthusiasm and he is so consumed by his commitments that he often lacks empathy and fails to attune himself to others.

Each sign has its strengths and weaknesses.

Aries, Leo, and Sagittarius use other people as fuel to feed their fire and to expand the extent of their will. Or they simply ignore others who do not share their commitments. So fire and will can be accomplished in a very positive way or equally in a very negative way.

The light changes, an individual steps off the curb to cross the street, and you grab that person's shirt and yank him back as a bus narrowly misses killing him in front of you. That is will-power in action in a positive way. You intervene and take control to protect life.

There is the guru sitting in his ashram smiling and content with lots of devotees who call him 'master.' But he takes no notice of the people dying out in the world around his ashram. He lacks the will to change the world. The pursuit of justice is not an ideal of his lineage. Or maybe that is why some of his students are attracted to him. They have been so burnt by fiery abuses of power that they need to retreat to a place of refuge where the only vibration in their minds is 'love and light.'

So basically, if you have power you are free to use that power. And with it, you get things done in the real world in a specific time frame. If you add wisdom to that power, then what you do is harmonious. If you add love, what you do heals and nurtures others. If you add the earth element with its sense of accomplishment and hard work, the results you produce are stable and enduring.

Politicians, on the other hand, often propose legislation that is ill-conceived because they have not tested their plans against reality. They have not done their homework so the results are poor. And also the key problem with politicians is that once elected they join an elect club and no longer represent the people who elected them. They are easily bribed by special interests.

Novice: So how do will and power actually relate to the fire element?

EQUIPOISE: INSIGHTS INTO FOUNDATIONAL ASTRAL TRAINING

Older Novice: Fire is hot, dry, intense, burning, commanding, urgent, demanding, consuming, exploding, and also illuminating. Different individuals burn with different levels of intensity and purity. Some of Hitler's generals possessed a will of steel. They were hardened in battle and brilliant in command.

But none of them could comprehend Hitler's will. Hitler was like a pyroclastic flow moving down a mountain at several hundred miles an hour and burning at two thousand degrees. And he was like a mountain exploding. The generals had never run into anything like this before. Having their own wills forced through experience in real situations in life, they could not conceive of a will that is purely negative and arising from the depths of archetypes.

So if you have been exposed to negative archetypal power, it is not just going to go away by embracing love and light. You can postpone the encounter, but at some point you will need to make peace with the archetypal and cosmic dragons that know your name and come calling from time to time to see if you are awake. In the end, you will need to embody in yourself the positive version of that negative cosmic power that has touched your life.

In some cases, in order to be prepared for an encounter with the fifth element of akasha, a magician lives for a time under the influence of a 'little dictator.' The negative alpha male micromanages and tries to control the person's actions, feelings, and mind. It takes an immense effort to retain one's own soul and will in such a situation and a supreme effort to break free of that alpha male's influence.

Sometimes, the will of that little dictator is actually cosmic in nature. And sometimes to purge yourself and become free of it you will need to identify with akasha itself – a formless void, where no fiery will exists by itself. There at last you attain freedom.

So it helps to be able to sense energy directly and to read auras. Otherwise sometimes people simply cannot believe what is happening. They go to their deaths not imagining that malice is ruling over them. So an individual with a great deal of will-power can bend or align others' wills to his own.

Novice: So there is something to be said for meditating on the many different kinds of man-made and natural fire in nature?

PART II: UNDERSTANDING MAGICAL EQUILIBRIUM

Older Novice: Absolutely. You can experience will from the inside so to speak. It is just that in applying that fire in a positive way will take real world experience.

Now then, are we done or do you want examples of how meditating on hot, fiery energy will develop will-power in yourself when you lack will-power? Like a solitary, introverted individual who has to appear in court and persuade a judge that his cause is right. He may drink coffee which he never drinks or eat meat even though he is a vegetarian to strengthen his will. But such rem-edies will no doubt be disastrous.

On the other hand, perhaps in arguing before the state board of education for a change in teacher union rules, he might imagine and practice speaking as if he is an Israeli general rehearsing for the last time a covert action they are going to take behind enemy lines.

Standing in front of a mirror, like an actor, he internalizes absolute confidence, calm courage, and precise clarity of expression. For the first time in his life he speaks with an electrifying voice because he imagines he is not himself but this battle-hardened general speaking to his own men who trust him with their lives.

And then he stands up at the state board of education meeting and speaks exactly as he has rehearsed. The room is so silent you can hear a pin drop. He gives a spell-binding performance and maybe in fact the state board of education is so impressed they do what he asks. Maybe they do so just because they do not want him coming back. The fire he exudes takes hold of them and they do not want to suffer again that intensity.

Novice: Ah. Right. I get it. Sometimes if done right, meditating on fire can expand your will-power but it takes a lot of rehearsing and practice to get it to be effective.

So there was just this little question in the back of my mind and I think it might apply here.

Older Novice: Yes. Go on.

Novice: What about male, female energies?
Older Novice: I was hoping you would not ask about that. I will try to be brief and concise though I know already I will fail in that attempt.

Here is the deal. The outraged feminists are right. For thousands of years, certainly going back eight thousand years, men have dominated and suppressed not just women but they have been at war with femininity itself. There is a real result. Feminine energy has been torn out of women on a collective level.

The entire global civilization at this point in history is all masculine. Edison, Tesla, and Westinghouse invented the electrical power grid. Every aspect of our lives has changed. Henry Ford came along with the Wright Brothers and used electrical motors to run their cars and airplanes. Without those advances in electricity, they would have had to fight WWI and WWII with horses instead of with mechanized infantry, tanks, and bombers.

Throw in Einstein and Oppenheimer and you now have the nuclear fire at the core of the sun appearing on earth. The Manhattan Project, the biggest project in this history of the world, was accomplished in three years and cities were destroyed by those bombs. Literally, some damn president can push a button during a crisis and unleash so much nuclear fire on earth the ozone layer is destroyed and you have a fair chance of the human race becoming extinct.

There is absolutely nothing in the feminine arsenal of soul abilities that is equivalent. The human race, if it is to survive, needs woman to be able to match masculine power on every front.

The modern world is all about fire. A man steps out on the street and the fiery and electrical inventions of his civilization amplifies his masculinity – the ability to take charge of and to control the world. Women demand equal access to this power, and the Patriarchal, alpha male-based, electrical civilization gives it to them contaminating, compromising, and completely co-opting the fem-inine powers within them.

This is after all what capitalism is good at – it co-opts its greatest critics, rewarding them with recognition, social status, and money. The critic then thinks she is being heard and points to changes made as a result of her actions. But the system smiles to itself and says, 'That was so easy. I have taken another barbarian and cloned her in my own image.'

It is not that the man has more male energy in his body and the woman has less feminine energy in her body. It is just that the path followed that leads to modern civilization has completely hidden what femininity is. A modern woman, now in so many ways freer, cannot accomplish the cosmic role assigned to femininity to contain, refine, transform, and direct male

PART II: UNDERSTANDING MAGICAL EQUILIBRIUM

energy. She has not a clue that those abilities are hidden deep inside of her soul.

Novice: Whoa. Wait a minute. You are saying that if I am trying to establish in my soul a balance between the four elements this is impossible to do unless I undertake some sort of extraordinary journey and join myself to original, primordial feminine energy? Is that what you are saying?

Older Novice: Not just me. Some of the mermaid queens declare that 'Unless you unite yourself from within to the feminine spirit all our gifts to you will be worthless.'

Novice: So you are saying that you can take this 'one size fits all' kind of Bardon student. And he looks at his list of positive and negative traits in his magic mirrors of the soul and says to himself, 'Ah. I am doing pretty good here. Balance attained. No more weak or negative traits.'

But all the same, without internalizing the energy of the opposite gender – the feminine essence – he will still be inevitably flawed.

Lacking empathy, clair-sentience, an inner, direct connection to nature, and pure innocence, he will remain a typical male – he will be narrow-minded because he clings to thoughts in order to think; he will be self-possessed because he has not learned to put his ego off to the side; he will be vain and selfish because he does not know how to give all of himself in every moment, and his will will be twisted because he does not have a clue how to join himself to fulfilling the deepest purposes of life. On and on.

Society has produced men who feel half dead inside to such an extent that in order to discover new things and find something exciting to do with themselves, they put their very existence at risk. The delight of the five senses and the feeling of being fully alive is not in them.

Older Novice: Yes. It is the water element that is missing from human civilization. The consciousness of actual mermaids as they exist on the astral plane with their innocent giving has never appeared in human literature, religion, or wisdom traditions. Thus without such knowledge and experience of water, astral equilibrium is an impossible venture – a trap lying in wait to deceive and ensnare young magicians everywhere.

EQUIPOISE: INSIGHTS INTO FOUNDATIONAL ASTRAL TRAINING

Novice: So what is your vision then? You talk about the feminine energy containing and directing masculine energy. That is the exact opposite of how the world has been set up where men dominate women and control women using them for support and an extra energy source to charge themselves up with a little sex.

Older Novice: It is in a later chapter of *Initiation into Hermetics*. The magnetic fluid – the essence of the feminine – like a ball, surrounds and contains the electric fluid at its center. The electric and magnetic are perfectly matched and harmoniously work together amplifying each other.

When done right, it is a natural feminine power all women possess deep inside themselves with complete ease, to join from within to any man on earth making him feel fully alive and fulfilling his deepest dreams.

Take Charles Dickens *Christmas Carol*. The masculine confrontation with Mr. Scrooge would be to just tell him point black with authority: 'Scrooge! You have to become a different man than who you are.'

And Scrooge would reply, 'Fuck off. It is my life. I will do with it what I want.'

You see, Scrooge is an impossible case. There is no way to get him to change. Why even bother?

But, little known to women on earth at this time, the feminine principle is infinite. All power and will is controlled by it.

A woman can so join with a man that when she speaks he hears his own voice speaking from the core of his being. She is a man's second conscience.

And so with subtlety, art, and high empathy, she enters Scrooge's dreams as the Ghosts of Past, Present, and Future. In her soul and mind, a woman can relive a man's own memories. She shows him his life as if he is gazing into a magic mirror.

'You do this right and the impossible occurs.' Scrooge thinks it is his own idea to change. He says to the Ghost of Christmas Future: 'Why show me this, if I am past all hope? Good Spirit, your nature intercedes for me, and pities me. Assure me that I yet may change these shadows you have shown me, by an altered life!'

A woman is closer to a man than his own breath and his own heartbeat. This is the power of the feminine that joins, unites, and transforms from within rather than through the ways of the external masculine world with its

PART II: UNDERSTANDING MAGICAL EQUILIBRIUM

competition, brute force, and massive exploitation of nature and of other people.

Novice: So what is the end goal of astral equilibrium? You make it sound as though pursuing astral equilibrium goes on forever.

Older Novice: The end goal or the provisional goal is to unite in your soul the kings and queens of the four elements. And this is no easy task. Right now the kings of the salamanders do not consult with mermaid queens when they oversee a super volcano erupting. The sylphs to not consult with the gnomes about the onset and ending of an ice age. But when this is accomplished, there will no longer be a separation between the four elements in nature. The biosphere of the planet itself will have one vibration of harmony.

Scientists may think they are engaged in pure research and furthering human understanding of nature. But their work is compromised and twisted by the corporations and governments that fund them. New scientific inventions almost immediately fall into the hands of the worst people on earth. The air element – scientists – is co-opted by the fire element – generals and presidents. There is no balance or harmony there.

Novice: So you are saying I need a woman in my life who is joined to nature at the core of her being and able to be so receptive she is free of all ego at least when she seeks to listen to her conscience or feel what is in her heart? Do such women even exist on earth?

Older Novice: A great many of the incarnated elemental beings who wear women's bodies are quite capable of loving in this way. In fact, when I interview some of them, what they have done for their male partners sounds exactly as if they were acting as the Ghosts of Christmas Past, Present, and Future. Being one hundred per cent receptive, being totally empathic and giving are not an affront to them. They are connected to nature from within and so do not seek constant reassurance by looking to others for self-validation.

Novice: So what do you do with human woman?

EQUIPOISE: INSIGHTS INTO FOUNDATIONAL ASTRAL TRAINING

Older Novice: If you practice *Initiation into Hermetics,* even in that first book, you are taught to enter the four elemental realms and learn all you can, making them into a second home. You just need a female magician who takes Bardon seriously. Or else a human woman who loves nature with all of her heart. The magic path and the path of the heart overlap in this area of connecting to nature from within.

Novice: Or else I need to get to know the water element so this empathic, receptive, and absolute giving and innocent energy is fully alive within myself.

PART II: UNDERSTANDING MAGICAL EQUILIBRIUM

5. E.Q.U.I.P.O.I.S.E. – ANGELICA DE LOS SANTOS

Exceptional
Quality
Underlying
Ideal
Performance
Of
Inner
Service
Elementally

Excellent
Qualification
Ultimately
Indicating
Possession
Of
Internal
Stable
Empowerment

Emancipating
Quadra-polar
Useful
Immunity
Protecting
Outstanding
Initiates
Serving
Earnestly

6. The Need for a Balanced Development – Ray del Sole

When we do introspection, then we can see that every one of us has a personal strength, special powers and abilities. So for example there are people with a great intellect, others have a powerful will or endurance, and others have a great intuition, maybe higher perception such as clairvoyance.

This is natural and normal. It is also normal that we are conditioned to use our personal strengths to make progress, to solve problems. So when you have a great intellect then you will probably use it to manage obstacles and challenges in your life. When your intuition is not well developed then you won't use it. This natural behavior maintains such imbalances in the personality.

Imagine a boxer who has a 'winner fist', his right hand. The boxer knows that with his right hand he can unfold great impacts so that it is most dangerous for his opponent to get in touch with it. But his left hand is quite weak. The boxer is focused only on his winner fist. His trainer knows about this imbalance. He forces him to do special training on his left hand. At first this training feels hard for the boxer because it is his weak hand and so it takes extra effort to make small progress. But after a while his left hand also becomes quite strong and dangerous. In the coming fight, the opponent is only focused on protecting himself from the right hand of the boxer, so the boxer cannot really hit the opponent with his right fist. But now, with his trained left hand, he is able to punch hard and so he wins the fight. He understands now how important equally trained fists are.

In the same way and even more comprehensively we are asked in the spiritual training to develop all powers, qualities and abilities equally as there are always situations in life where we cannot make any progress with our favorite strength. Additionally, the law of harmony is also in charge as we strive for higher and the highest balance in our nature.

Practically speaking this means that we should consciously train our weaker aspects to develop them.

Turn weakness into strength! Then we can enjoy life even more as more doors open and more ways are available to face the challenges of life.

The more we unfold, the more beauty we can experience.

PART II: UNDERSTANDING MAGICAL EQUILIBRIUM

7. Some Aspects of Magical Equilibrium – Ray del Sole

Somehow life is all about balancing and the magical equilibrium is the highest aspect of it. I think a good and easy approach to this topic is physics. When you take a pencil and balance it on your finger or when you think of a pendulum then you get good insights why balancing is so important and what the effects are of being in balance or not. When you examine life and behavior then it is really like a pendulum which swings from one side – extreme – to the other side until it reaches total balance in the center. Here you can see that nearly the same amount of energy is used to swing from one side to the other while passing the point of balance, the center. It is also an aspect of karma. For example, let's say you do something wrong in life. With the same intensity of energy you used to do it, you have to balance your bad behavior. Here's a different example: the amount of need for relaxation is analogous to the amount needed for doing sports. So indeed, the pendulum tells a lot about balance, balancing and karma.

If you like martial arts, then you know how important it is to be centered – to be in balance. Only when you are centered will you be able to make all the moves you need/wish for. When you are not centered, your moves are very limited.

Balance is an aspect of God. God sits always in the center. Dynamic balancing or imbalance is an aspect of life and creation. We are all in a permanent dynamic balancing process. It is the change of polarities. It is rhythm.

So you meet God in the center, the stillness and not outside.

In life this means that you are and feel centered, centered in yourself, the master attitude. Being centered means to be able to act in all imaginable ways without limitations, limitations caused by imbalance. It means freedom, power, concentration, flexibility but also inner peace and in-dependence, it means time to think before you act or react. It means a growing mastership in life and a good connection to God.

Magical balancing comes along with saturation with all elements. So you feel saturated, you are a part of the natural-divine cornucopia. Needs and wishes decrease to a minimum.

It is the Indian sattva state while the world is in rajas and some people live in tamas.

For the magical equilibrium, the work with the elements is important as you reach a state of balance which is beyond human possibilities. This means that meditation and soul mirror work is good but the energetic work, with vital energy and especially the four elements, is a very important aspect with very important effects. It means clearing/washing of the soul and it means saturation with all necessary energies.

Certainly, you increase your level of energy and charisma by all these works as a side effect and also your success in life will increase automatically. And last but not least, you will appear more beautiful and harmonious because of the changes in your aura.

PART II: UNDERSTANDING MAGICAL EQUILIBRIUM

8. LET'S HAVE DINNER – ERIC SUMMERS

Balance Within
Balance Without
Balance it now or forever live in doubt

Let's have dinner at a four-legged table
Balanced on the level, knowing that it's stable

Let's have conversations that can't be heard
Let's dine and talk without saying a word

Let's talk to Gods and travel the planes
Use Divine Letters like scrabble with flames

Let's become gods in the shape of a man
Control elemental forces with the wave of a hand

Let's do our best, Let's be great
Let's Create Our Destiny
Let's Change our Fate

Balance it now for before it's late
The Heavenly calendar knows our date
The Scales of Justice knows our weight
Let's strive to do good for goodness sake

Birth our love and kill our hate
Balance our Table to hold our plates

Let's have dinner

9. What is Magic Equilibrium? –Richard A. Wright

The first step to adepthood is self-knowledge. The Temple of Apollo, the site of the Oracle of Delphi, had inscribed over its entrance 'Know Yourself'. This maxim is the cornerstone of magic.

The magician must be intimately familiar with his or her own traits, characteristics, emotions and personality. Magic equilibrium occurs when the personality as a whole has attained a harmonic balance between four elements so that the fifth element may be conducted at its optimum efficiency. When a person attains complete self-knowledge and self-awareness and is able to retain complete conscious control over themselves, then that person has achieved what psychoanalysts refer to as 'synthesis'. The practitioner has encountered all aspects of themselves and allowed them to form a harmonious union. This is also the purpose of Yoga – to bring the body and mind under conscious control, or to 'yoke' the unconscious which allows a state of union to occur.

There is a Hermetic saying 'that which is within is like that which is without'. Let us imagine for a moment that reality does not exist in an objective way. Instead imagine that it is like a three-dimensional blank canvas. Inside your head is a projector, so when you look around the blank canvas you actually see it as the reality that you are familiar with, complete with tables and chairs and trees and pavements. What makes reality appear real is actually a program in your head that shapes your reality. If you are somehow able to change the programming that has gone into your head, and you build a harmonious persona, your external reality will change accordingly. This is the microcosm aligning with the macrocosm – there is an objective reality, and this is what the Hindus refer to as Ultimate Reality. Or Brahman – the ineffable face of God. The practice of mysticism was to cultivate the inner realm so that it aligned with the divine and the practitioner would achieve direct conscious union with God. The Abrahamic religions mention this by stating that God created (hu)man in his own image. In other words, we have the potential to achieve equality with God.

Let us consider the weapons at the magician's disposal. The disc, represents Earth. This is the foundation upon which the magician will base his or her work. The disc must be represented within. Bills and debts must be

PART II: UNDERSTANDING MAGICAL EQUILIBRIUM

paid in full and on time. Words spoken must be followed through with action. Your character must carry weight. The cup, represents emotions. This is the importance of feeling. If you become emotionally detached then you are losing a fundamental part of your humanity: empathy. Being able to empathize with others, including non-human consciousness, is very important to the magician's work. The sword, representative of intellect – you must be intelligent to be a magician. You must read, study, learn and do so in an active environment to hone your intellect until it is razor sharp. And the wand – representative of fire – the magician's will. Doing anything that requires will-power, whether it's doing your household chores, going to work, giving up smoking or climbing mount Everest, generates energy. When you succeed in your goals this too begets still more energy, translating these symbols into personal characteristics which are Persistence, Empathy, Wisdom and Volition.

Until you have the traits mentioned above the magic simply will not work. You may be able to achieve certain results to a certain degree, but Bardon's analogy of a key is very apt. Equilibrium is a literal key that unlocks the true power of your mind. Upon achieving equilibrium, the results will speak for themselves – you will seldom get sick. You will find you have large amounts of physical energy. You can achieve contact with your supra-consciousness, the 'knowledge and consciousness of your Holy Guardian Angel.' The HGA is the aspect of your consciousness that you are trying to awaken with these exercises – make no mistake this is not an external consciousness, the HGA is you, just a more refined, more intelligent higher aspect.

A Christian priest and a Buddhist monk were drinking tea together one day discussing their respective religions. The Buddhist was attempting to explain meditation on no thought as a practice and the priest responded that Christian Prayer was similar except that the conscious awareness focused on God. Three times this happened when the monk tried to explain a subtlety of his practice and the priest always likened it to his own practices. Then the monk picked up the teapot and started pouring tea into the priest's cup although it was already full. As the tea overflowed onto the table the priest cried in surprise and alarm 'What are you doing?' The monk calmly responded 'You see how difficult it is to fill your cup when yours is already full?' The point the monk was making is that in order to change your personality, you have to get rid of your old personality. You wish to become enlightened? Then you have to go.

How much of your mind is influenced by adverts and television? Is your cultural upbringing influencing your decisions? Are these your thoughts or are they your friends' and family's thoughts? Does your favorite movie character influence your behavior? These are all things that the practitioner must discover.

Who is to say what constitutes positive and negative? Whose code of ethics are we following? How do we define objectively what constitutes good and bad? Traditionally, religion has provided moral guidance, but this is fraught with problems for the magician. The magician will view religion as being twofold – an exterior structure around which the mystical aspect will cling like ivy climbing a golden bough. Therefore the main religion will not contain the requisites necessary for direct communion with the divine. Bardon's system contains these requisites without the need for external religion, but do not underestimate the power of ritual and symbols especially when communicating with the unconscious. The student of Bardon should therefore be familiar with the external practices of all world religions, and even engage in their rituals.

Another problem with behavior alteration is that the practitioner is the lab, the test subject and the scientist conducting the test all at the same time. And since the test subject is a dynamic being, as you encounter yourself you start to build up an awareness of who you are. As you build up this picture, you start to recognize what your strengths and weaknesses are and you start to manage them, so that your strengths are maximized and your shortcomings are minimized. This is the essence of self-awareness – avoid situations that bring out the worst in you. Enter situations where you can use your strengths. In due time, your altered behavior becomes habit. It takes approximately three weeks to establish a behavior pattern. The idea is that you establish behavior patterns with the assistance of conscious eating breathing and drinking. If the practitioner makes the conscious intention for their necessities into one intention, the results will be magnified. For example, you wish to cultivate patience because you have ascertained that impatience is the root trait that brings about many other negative traits. When impatience is tempered with patience, then drive and diligence is the result. The impatience has as its positive attribute that of drive, and so we see that each attribute has

PART II: UNDERSTANDING MAGICAL EQUILIBRIUM

positive and negative aspects. So drink patience, eat patience, breathe patience for three weeks, and the resulting characteristic will soon manifest.

When psychoanalysts discuss synthesis, they use the analogy of a waterfall. In other words disparate aspects of the psyche achieve union despite their differences. The psyche is better understood as similar to having multiple personalities. Your work persona should be different from your home persona or your social persona. Are you the same person to your family as you are to your colleagues? Almost all of us will have cultivated different personas in order to function in society. But how conscious are you of your different personas? Are they in conflict with one another? This is a key question and the answer will help greatly in establishing equilibrium.

Mind your surroundings. Where you live, where you work, where you socialize all play a role in your personality. Are you happy in your job? Are your friends good people? Are you happy with where you live? These are all important questions because they all contribute to your mental input. The subconscious mind is the key to all magic, and it is constantly soaking up the input that you give it, including your own auto-suggestion, that you may or may not be aware you are doing.

How many of us have gone into work on a Monday morning thinking to ourselves 'I don't want to be here.'? This contributes to your unhappiness greatly, whereas if you're thinking to yourself 'time to earn my living' it can be much easier. This is to do with cultivating the right attitude. If you have a positive approach to obstacles, problems and setbacks, then you will solve them much quicker with a positive mind set. Remember your subconscious only understands positive statements. This is why it so difficult to quit smoking – you can't say 'don't smoke' to yourself because you have to think of the thing you want to remove. Too late you already thought about smoking. A better alternative mantra might be 'I want to breathe clearly'. The subconscious mind is childish in that it will try to sabotage the practitioner and bring about self-sabotaging behavior.

This is the reason Bardon starts with this aspect of the work, and this is why it's so important. If you have direct control of your subconscious mind then you have achieved enlightenment. If you have not and you enter into magical ritual, then you can create a great many problems, because your subconscious may do exactly the opposite of your desired result.

So how do we get to that stage? The diary is key here. The order in which you conduct the introspection is important. The categorizing of elements to each character trait is vital. Start with negative traits. Write down AT LEAST a hundred. Yes, a hundred. You need that many to form an accurate picture. You need a hundred positive ones as well, and this is why it's vital you complete this task. After you have torn yourself down, by listing a hundred negative traits within two weeks, you then build yourself back up with a hundred positive traits. This leaves you feeling confident and validated. The process of writing them down has a magic in itself, because you are naming your aspects, and by naming them you gain control over them.

Sometimes conscious awareness of a trait is enough to alter it. Some people complain that they are struggling to find so many traits about themselves. This is where Tarot and astrology can be employed. With astrology, I am not talking about a horoscope in the paper, but an in-depth look at your natal chart, in which you will need not only your date of birth but the hour of your birth. Planetary consciousness does play a role in human behavior – the moon exerts its influence on the earth by means of the tides, Jupiter and Saturn act as a firmament to keep Earth in a balanced orbit, the asteroid belt helps to act as an asteroid safety net. On a more subtle level though there are planetary energies that pervade the solar system, and the hour of your birth will have certain energies at work which will transmit a certain vibration that will resonate with the practitioner.

As Bardon's training progresses you will encounter elemental breathing, elemental accumulation and eventually creation of magical beings. Without creating the proper conditions, namely equilibrium, these beings will not manifest, or if they do, the practitioner is at risk of possession and/or obsession. Bardon's requirement is that you train your mind, body and soul at the same time. The exercises he lays out complement each other and each aspect, if properly directed, can greatly assist in other aspects. For example, thought observation, conscious eating, auto-suggestion and behavior alteration all paint different aspects of the complete picture. These initial steps are taught early with the expectation that you revisit these exercises frequently so as to gauge your development.

To consciously achieve magic equilibrium the practitioner requires complete self-awareness and self-control. It is a never-ending process that alters as you progress. At its fundamental core it is the very essence of the magician's great work. Cultivating your inner realm so that it is harmonious and balanced will allow the divine conduits to flow easily and will ultimately

PART II: UNDERSTANDING MAGICAL EQUILIBRIUM

balance your karma and progress your spiritual evolution into the next stage of human development.

Part III: Establishing Magical Equilibrium

PART III: ESTABLISHING MAGICAL EQUILIBRIUM

1. Active Imagination Technique: Dear Subconscious, Let's Be Friends? – J.L. Amato

Part I: The Cards We Have Been Given

We live in a society where there is no systematic teaching given to everyone at an early age, focused in helping to prevent, understand and overcome different types of emotional suffering.

Although there are exceptions, in general our schools do not have disciplines that deal with this subject, much less in the depth that it requires and deserves.

Considering this context, it is no surprise that there is a huge number of people who suffer from depression, excessive anxiety and stress, low self-esteem, difficulties in socialization and relationships and other issues.

Part II: Introduction To The Active Imagination Technique

What if you could have access to any part of your personality, ways of thinking, feeling and behaving, even if it was a very deep and unconscious part, and you could understand it, and transform it in the direction you want?

Sounds a bit utopic, right? Fortunately, it's very real. However, like many things in life, this one also demands some level of perseverance and hard work, if you want to have very good results with it.

But let's go to the starting point, and travel through this chapter together. Psychologist Carl Jung, in 1935, used the term active imagination for the first time in public, to refer to the methodology he was applying to himself and to his patients.

Through conscious intention, in a conscious state, each person is able to trigger their subconscious mind into spontaneously producing different types of symbols – images, sounds, sensations, characters, objects, scenarios, and others – to manifest in the imagination, represent the desired form of thinking, feeling and behaving that the person is seeking to understand or transform.

PART III: ESTABLISHING MAGICAL EQUILIBRIUM

By interacting with the symbols that appear in their mind, the person is able to understand the psychological dynamic in question, gathering information that could have taken a long time to be collected. Different strategies can be applied to transform the inner content that has manifested.

Perhaps a few examples could bring more color to our journey here and make the essence of the technique more clear. Let's say someone feels a mysterious sadness and they do not know its origin. Such sadness could be directed to manifest in the imagination, as a symbol – for example a character searching to understand the message behind the sadness, why it is there. By understanding the message, different routes could be taken.

Or let's say someone rationally, consciously, thinks that a certain idea, for example a pessimistic view of the world, doesn't make any sense. Still, in certain situations, that same idea and connected feelings and behaviors, manifest themselves, bringing trouble and suffering to this person. In this scenario, on a subconscious level, this person still believes in the idea he is trying to get rid of. There is a polarization in the mind about this subject, and through the active imagination, it is possible to access the subconscious part that still believes in the pessimist view, and transform it.

One of the advantages of the active imagination is that you do not need to be feeling the specific feeling you want to work with. You can access it, even if you are not feeling it in this exact second.

The same applies to forms of thinking. If in this moment certain negative thoughts don't make sense for you or you are not 'buying into them', you can still access the part of you that does believe.

The technique itself is simple, but let's look into some important details first.

III: Preparations and Warnings

Although it is possible to dive directly into the active imagination, certain previous and basic preparations seem to be of benefit, helping to more easily achieve the experience, especially for people who are learning the basics of the technique. I will describe them, and in sequence provide the basic model for the technique containing them.

There are special preparations that can be made, which I will describe below as well. They are not required for the technique itself, but especially when dealing with great sufferings, traumas or inner blocks, they help a lot, by making the experience easier to deal with, less intense, and in overcoming certain initial resistances, so that the person feels more motivated to continue using the technique.

If you are feeling insecure, afraid, or in doubt about all of this, I specially recommend the use of the Fractionation preparation.

A) Warnings

If you are having suicidal thoughts or any form of hallucinations, you should not use this technique without the support of someone very familiar with its functioning and with dealing with emotional sufferings. Alone, without a greater experience in the technique, and in understanding specific sufferings, there is a great risk that, with those emotional dynamics happening, you would bring more to the surface of something you are probably not ready to completely deal with in the moment, which may lead to a negative intensification of the situation.

B) Basic Preparation: Creating a Rational and Conscious Foundation

If you wish only to understand a psychological dynamic, but not to transform it, this preparation is not necessary. Still, for people learning the basics, I recommend making use of this preparation.

However, if you wish to transform or overcome something, this is a requirement. Without this foundation, the technique won't produce the transformation you are seeking, and depending on the emotional content you are accessing, there is a chance you will end up feeling worse after using it – the reasons will be clear as we advance.

This preparation is about consciously and rationally/logically, questionimg the chosen form of thinking, feeling or behaving, to see if we believe this is the best way to handle whatever is happening.

If this initial reflection is not done, when the active imagination is used, the person would be entering in contact with a part of themselves that believes in the same thing her conscious/rational mind believes. In this scenario, there is no polarization, two different points of view, and transformations will not be taking place, since the consciousness is not ready to bring a new point of view to transform the old one.

An example can make this preparation more clear. Let's say you are feeling guilty about something you have done. If you consciously and rationally think it is reasonable for you to feel guilty concerning such a situation, that you should feel guilty, then you will continue to feel guilty. By using the active imagination to enter into contact with your guilt, you will manifest a part that has the same opinion as your conscious/rational point of view. No transformation is possible here.

However, if you question the reasons behind your guilt, and realize that in such a situation you have done all that was possible with the physical, emotional and mental resources that were available to you, then, at least on a conscious and rational level, the guilt begins to lose strength – although you may still feel it. In this point, there is a polarization, two different points of view in your mind. With such a rational position established, your consciousness is ready to bring the same reflection to the more subconscious part of you, that still believes the guilt is reasonable, and that leads you to feel that way. The possibility of transforming such a part, by convincing it of the new point of view, becomes real.

To help you in this rational questioning, talking to other people about the subject, researching it online or in books, watching videos about other points of view, are examples of paths that can inspire you in this process.

C) Basic Preparation: Entering into a State of Relaxation

This is not necessary for the technique, but it may help people who are learning it, since it will make it easier for them to bring their attention into their own minds with fewer distractions.

Take a few breaths, slowly inspiring and expiring, feeling the air entering and leaving your body. Use the time you feel necessary.

If the person thinks she will fall asleep or that she will become sleepy, this relaxation should be left aside. To better enjoy this experience, the person should be conscious and in an alert state.

EQUIPOISE: INSIGHTS INTO FOUNDATIONAL ASTRAL TRAINING

D) Basic Preparation: Creating Inner Scenarios – Safe and Welcoming Environments

This is also not necessary to the technique itself, but helps people to start having their experiences in an inner environment that is more welcoming and perhaps familiar.

Imagine yourself in a place where you feel confident, at peace and safe. You may choose the place, or allow your mind to manifest one for you spontaneously, based on the choice of feelings. Some people imagine themselves in their own bedrooms or in the middle of nature, such as forests or mountains.

In other uses of the technique, more detailed ones, this inner scenario can be a place to perform other preparations before entering into contact with a certain emotional content.

E) Special Preparation: Fractionation of the Emotional Charge

Entering into contact with something that is terrifying for us, or hard to deal with, can be difficult.

What if we could enter into contact with ten percent of its emotional intensity or charge? What about one percent? Or even less? Sounds much easier to deal with, right? This special preparation helps to do exactly that.

One way to apply it, is to desire for a door to appear in the imagination or in the inner scenario you created. Then, to imagine a percentage appearing in the door, for example ten percent, as if it was written on its surface.

Finally, to desire that on the other side of this door, only ten percent, in this example, of that part we are trying to enter into contact with, will appear. And that's it. Let your mind do the rest.

F) Special Preparation: Using Inner Allies

To deal with our sufferings alone, can sometimes be difficult. This preparation helps with that, by creating different forms of support to aid us in our inner journey.

For example, positive ideas or positive feelings such as confidence, optimism, peace, can appear in the imagination as characters, objects, or even entire scenarios. We may also imagine people who we know, with whom we feel safe. Some people imagine someone from their family, or a friend, or their therapist.

G) Special Preparation: The Light of the Self

Our mind and emotional structure has the potential of expressing all possible personality characteristics to a human being, even if in the moment we do not possess them, or even if we never had them.

This potential can be expressed as a symbol in the imagination, in the form of a light, energy or force. For example, we can imagine it as a colored smoke, whatever color we prefer, energy or light, representing that potential. It can also manifest as a character or object that we carry with us. When dealing with chaotic images, this 'light' can help to stabilize things or give us strength to face them.

Part IV: Basic Model for using the Active Imagination

Read all the instructions below, so you won't have to interrupt the experience in the middle to remember any detail. If you are only going to try to understand an issue and not to transform it or overcome it, skip non-related parts.

If you have already created a rational foundation about the theme you plan to work with, put yourself in a comfortable position. Perform the breathing exercise, to enter into a relaxation state. Then, imagine yourself in the safe and welcoming environment. Initially, it will be easier to do this and perform the technique with your eyes closed.

Observe this place in your imagination. In some point of it, there will be a door, or a door will appear. Don't open it yet. At this moment, perform any special preparations you may wish to use.

When you are ready, desire that on the other side of this door there will be a part of you, a form of feeling, thinking or behaving, that you wish to understand and/or transform.

Now, desire that such a part will appear behind the door, in the form of a character or something that you will be able to interact with – you can talk to anything in the imagination, objects, environments, and other things. Don't seek to control the experience, just desire and let your mind choose the form of this symbol.

It will not necessarily be visual. It may be acoustic, like a 'voice'/thought in your mind, or a sensation in your body.

Now, open the door and enter the space of this character, symbol, or desire for it to enter your space. What impression does this symbol, this part of you, give to you? Try to talk with this character; see if it needs anything, how you can help it. If you already know what this character/symbol stands for, ask why he believes in that or why he is feeling a certain way. Be persistent.

When it presents its point of view to you, try to convince it of something different, more constructive, using your rational foundation. Bring your reflections to this character.

This verbal convincing may lead the appearance of the character and/or the environment around it to change. This is a good sign. Don't worry if it takes time; some emotional contents may take a long time to transform. If you become tired, focus your attention in your body, in your breathing, open your eyes, and seek to do the technique in another moment.

Another useful option is the use of visual resources to gather information. For this, ask the character to show you, in a mirror, screen or surface, when that form of thinking, feeling or behaving started or something that helps you understand it more.

A very versatile visual resource is the use of associations through colors, to help in the transformation of a certain emotional content. To make use of this 'trick', first, wonder which color, for you, would be associated with the perspective, idea, characteristic, you wish to bring to the part you are accessing in the imagination.

For example, if you are accessing the part of you that has a pessimist view, and you wish to visually bring to it the rational construction of optimism that you have created in your previous reflections, then this optimistic view could appear in the imagination as a color of your choice. Don't think too much; just let your mind suggest a color.

This color can manifest as a colored smoke, gas, light or energy, or whatever way you prefer. Then, imagine this energy concentrating itself, being absorbed and incorporated by the character or symbol that represents the pessimistic view, transforming it. Try to keep the visualization going for some time, of this energy being continuously absorbed by the character, as though it was flowing from an infinite source.

Such methodology produces a reframing, a transformation, of conscious and/or subconscious emotional contents. It is also possible to use this resource in acoustic, sensorial or other ways, that would produce an equal transformation.

Part V: Dealing with Expectations, Priorities and Apparent Lack of Results/Blocks

It may take a long time to transform completely certain forms of thinking, feeling or behaving. Some of them have many related aspects and may have traumatic roots. It is a construction – or a de-construction – that you are doing here. Don't give up and you will definitely succeed in it. Having a more flexible expectation, that things may not happen in the speed you are thinking, will help avoid frustration.

With time and experience, as with many things in life, this inner work also has a tendency to become easier. Through active imagination, you will enlarge your knowledge of yourself and the functioning of the human personality traits, which will boost the entire process, as a cycle. Take notes of essential information, especially in the beginning; they may save you a lot of time and suffering in the future

Still, it may happen that a certain issue, even one that causes you great suffering, may be transformed quickly.

Having priorities and regularity in working with the chosen inner character/symbols, is essential to greater results. Build a 'map' of your positive and negative personality characteristics and choose strategically from there. Don't worry, with time your choices of what to focus on will get better.

Sometimes, you will open a door in the imagination, seeking to meet a part of yourself, and there won't be anything manifested there or you won't feel comfortable to open or enter the door. Don't worry. Ask yourself, are you afraid of meeting this part? Reflect about this, and walk towards feeling more confident about such an encounter; a greater fractionation can help here. You can put aside this encounter and focus first on meeting the fear related to the encounter.

Initially, you don't need to open the door. Try to talk to the part you want to meet, without seeing it, and bring through small openings in the door a certain energy to this part that you believe will transform it. With time, you will win confidence and will open the door.

Another possibility, to deal with the 'block' situation – where nothing appears behind the door, or you feel afraid to enter/open it – is to wonder what type of relationship you have to your own emotions/feelings, thoughts and inner world as a whole. Remember they necessarily have constructive roles and are always sending you messages. Try to be open to the message and don't try to control things when you desire for something to manifest. And whatever issue you are working with necessarily can be transformed, overcome, so you can be optimistic about it.

The emotional content you are manifesting as a character or symbol may stay in silence. If this happens, spend time with it, seeing if something appears in your mind. Significant insights can occur during active imagination. Passing confidence to this part of you, saying that everything can be understood and transformed, can help it to open up, but only if, at least rationally, you believe this. Anther possibility is to embrace it, hold its hands. For some people, this sensorial contact can help.

Part VI: Suggestions and the World of Possibilities

An enormous number of variations and possibilities could be used and explored through the active imagination technique. Due to lack of space, I shall mention very briefly some of them:

- Working with Dreams and Nightmares: in a conscious, daily state, you can access part or all of the emotional content of a dream or a nightmare. Don't miss the important messages your unconscious is sending during the night

- Active Imagination during lucid dreams: you may interact and transform emotional contents inside the lucid/conscious dream state, in the same way that you would do during the active imagination.

PART III: ESTABLISHING MAGICAL EQUILIBRIUM

- The Persona or 'Social Mask': perhaps sometimes you wear a 'mask' that you do not want to wear? This theme is associated with many aspects of our socialization and daily life.

- Inner Hero (or similar variants): we all have, or can have, deeper objectives, and we may or not be connected to them, walking the journey associated to them. The Inner Hero can represent this theme.

- Counsel from the Wise Old Man: ever wanted to receive counsel from a part of you that may have realized something you haven't realized yet? Well, manifest that part and see what it has to say.

- The Feminine, Masculine, and different forms of identity and expression: it is also possible to access, at the same time, a set of related emotional contents, for example, to access my relation to the 'masculine' or to the 'feminine'. This may provide interesting experiences that can be explored, later, as individual characteristic as well.

- Focusing on entire relations with unknown people, colleagues, friends, family or sexual/love partners: in the same way as the above, you can manifest everything about a certain relation in a symbol or character.

- The Inner Child: perhaps you have lost contact with a part of yourself, due to the pressures and responsibilities that appeared? You can reconnect with those parts, bringing them to the present moment.

- The Clues of the Unconscious: working on our emotional equilibrium can be quite complex. Why not ask our own mind to show us what part of us is missing or needs to be worked on, so we can feel more 'ourselves' and happier?

- It is Gifts Day! Why not ask, in the imagination, to receive something – a tip, a clue, so we can advance – from a part of us we are trying to connect to or understand more?

- Working with specific memories: sometimes, it can be difficult to transform certain forms of thinking, feeling or behaving, without dealing with the emotional charge of specific memories that may have caused a big impact on us, consciously and/or unconsciously. Use your imagination to enter into certain memories and transform the meaning you are now taking from them.

- Working with the 'Shadow': there may be parts of ourselves that we do not consciously identify with and that we don't believe exist inside of us. Still, sometimes, they do exist and can silently cause great problems, directly or indirectly. Meeting those parts may feel like a surprise and/or give a feeling of something strange. Don't be afraid when you meet them in your inner journeys; just seek to integrate them in a constructive way.

- Inner Meeting: if there seems to be great conflict between parts of yourself, why not gather everyone in the same room in the imagination, listen to them, so you can understand the motivation behind their manifestations/expressions, and then seek a constructive arrangement among all parts involved?

- My starting point is my Art: our artistic expression, physical or not, can have very strong ties to specific emotional aspects. Those images can be used in the active imagination.

- Very Quick Active Imagination while in the middle of daily activities: if you don't have any time in a certain moment, and you are having emotions and thoughts that are bringing you trouble, desire for them to manifest in a symbol in the imagination. And that's it; don't work with the image, do it another time. Sometimes this manifestation produces an emotional processing that *temporarily* makes things easier to deal with.

Part VII: Final Comments

Writing this brought me great joy, due to the special role this technique has played and continues to play, in my life.

PART III: ESTABLISHING MAGICAL EQUILIBRIUM

This technique, and its many variations and possibilities, are not a topic much talked about, taught or researched in Psychology with the necessary depth. I hope that, in a not far away future, I will finish writing a systematic book about this subject, detailing more its possibilities and sharing many examples, related to overcoming different sufferings – depression, anxiety, low self-esteem, anger, laziness, and many others – to better illustrate this subject.

One day, possibly, students in school will learn this subject, and will be able to prevent much suffering. They will have the tools to build bridges towards the subconscious and build a healthy and constructive relationship toward their inner world. This, necessarily, will change the relationship with the outer world.

I dedicate this chapter to everyone who supported me, in different ways, visibly, or, in other cases, more subtly. Certainly, without them, much of who I am today would not be.

A special mention to the few ones, who, in specific moments of my life, refused to give me answers or transform my issues for me, even when I was suffering a lot. They gave me the chance to build the inner pieces that would lead me to becoming who, deeply, I wanted to be. I believe that without such moments, this chapter and the book that will eventually come, would not be possible. Thank you.

If I may be of help to those who read this or if you would like to share your inner adventures, feel free to contact me.

2. The Magic of Water – Angel of God

When the Tao Te King says something like: 'Water is the element closest to the Tao' that is true. Water by its taciturn, balanced, sweet and generous nature, is certainly the element closest to the absolute.

The absolute is not outside our cosmos, outside our galaxy, but inside ourselves. In fact, you think they are inside of whom?

Water teaches us many virtues and those virtues need to be remembered and practiced. Water has life as its primary function, because without it no life is possible. In fact, even fire would not exist without water and if we go a little deeper into this question, what would be of Yang without Yin?

But more than philosophies it is necessary to bring and to clarify what is magic. For some magic is 'the art of bringing changes' or even 'the faculty of performing miracles', but all this is just an exaggeration: the true miracles are much more discreet and simple than they can imagine.

When the flames of daily problems are consuming us and despairing us, a glass of fresh water and a prayer can do what some rituals of this world can, and I can tell you that water can give us hope, hope that better days will come, that no matter how infernal the problem is, there is always hope.

Now imagine, if your body is seventy percent water and your mind only vibrates with hatred and despair, what do you think will happen to your health? The water as a universal fluidic condenser, able to attract and hold any nature of element or thought – what do you think will happen to your body in time?

Be careful what you think and be even more careful what you say. For the evil that vibrates on its own slowly destroys you. But the evil that you direct at others can often be the drop of water.

Perhaps you find it strange that the title of this text says 'The magic of water' and you think 'Here there must be a magic formula for some problem of mine' or 'Maybe I'll find out how to satisfy this or that whim' or even worse things.

PART III: ESTABLISHING MAGICAL EQUILIBRIUM

If you want to learn the magic of water, remember its virtues and practice them; stop choosing the wide door, stop choosing the easy path, shortcuts that will not take you anywhere.

Do you want to have the gift of making rains? Do you want the gift of healing your brothers with teas and other magic elixirs based on water? Then remember to practice your virtues!

Water is nothing more than a holy and blessed virtue, a cosmic characteristic. If we are going to think about the qualities of water, I ask you to remember the greatest of all mothers, the mothers of mothers, who carried the cosmic spark in their womb, the master of all masters, the master of all mercy, our lord the Christ.

In his uterus full of amniotic fluid, there was a frequency, an energetic power outside of all human and even inhuman patterns and conceptions, of his sweet womb, the greatest of all rested quietly, in peace.

Not that he himself was not peace, but also that his mother Mary, savior of the renegades, queen of mercy and mother of the unfortunate, had the grace and the capacity to receive the greatest of all, because in his being, all the virtues in maximum degree of understanding were there, mainly the water. She alone was a cosmic example of docility, a characteristic that is indispensable of water for you humans to live.

When Mary spoke, she spoke so sweetly, so kindly that the birds and plants were entertained, her delicate, firmer walk inspired everything and everyone. She also taught that the woman does not need the exaggerations and lack of control of fire and earth, but the intelligence of the air and the serenity of water.

Her touch was delicate enough for the greatest of the brutes, to run out to cry, her eyes were ineffable and pure, not even the waters of paradise were as pure as her sweet gaze.

If you knew how many evil ones had already been converted by her simple presence or even how many tragedies, thanks to her mercy they were supplanted.

The water, my brethren, contains mysteries that go even beyond my capacities, but I tell you, if you truly want to perform miracles and be recognized by the elemental queens of the waters, or even be blessed by the angelic principalities, begin with the basic, begin with sweetness, with

EQUIPOISE: INSIGHTS INTO FOUNDATIONAL ASTRAL TRAINING

forgiveness, with gentleness and then with all certainty even greater mysteries will be presented to you.

PART III: ESTABLISHING MAGICAL EQUILIBRIUM

3. To See Each Life Opportunity as a Lecture and a Possibility to Transform your Trait – Johannes Kul

'At this very present moment I'm writing this sentence to myself because this is the time when I realized that, until now I've never been happier and more satisfied than I am now – being aware of my own success and comprehending my whole life progress. Looking forward to continue breathing in it.'

One day I wrote myself this note instantly, with pure honesty, while I just sat there in my room, lying on a bed, reading a book during a muggy day. For a second I paused the book and just started contemplating my tough childhood and everything I've been through, comparing my current life, living place, job, hobbies and people I love. I actually realized that I had just done my second Introspection, unknowingly, being happy and aware of magical unfolding that continued to expand.

When I started with self-transformation work I always asked myself: 'How am I going to behave, feel and think after few months of it? How am I going to interact with people in general? How are people going to accept me in such expansion? Are they going to think that I'm a new person now? What if one of my black mirror traits becomes even worse? What if I disappoint all the people I really love?' A few months later I never thought about those questions again. My life changed drastically. Each life decision was a part of transformation.

That transformation influenced my point of view and perspective of IIH Step 2. I stopped constantly thinking and writing everything about it. I learned to relax and breathe in it – to live simultaneously with self-introspection and transformation.

At first, I've always had a strict plan. I gave a name to this plan, like a codename, because I always needed some kind of short code to never forget about my plan, so that I could write it everywhere – my own plan of transformation. It had the whole so-called IIH daily protocol.

But later came the thought of bad establishment. I thought I didn't need that codename anymore, because my dis-remembering and uncertainty could get worse. Then I finally realized and found a black sheep in a flock – I was afraid of forgetting stuff. Sounds familiar? Yeah, I found another deep black mirror trait to get rid of, which was actually much bigger than I thought.

So I decided to focus on remembering things. It felt like a life without a smartphone. Because with our smartphones we have enough services to make us lazy and forgetful. That's why I tried to stay focused on re-membering things and I've also tried to use a smartphone and all similar objects as little as possible. In the meantime my memory improved, because I was also trying to learn some new things in my life, like programming language and few coding tricks, where my memory needs to be a bit sharper, to memorize all of those logical operations. I wasn't even sure if I was going to continue with programming in my life, but you never know until you try – at least some useful life experience.

I decided to continue with using 7-Pronged Attack, with full force. Now comes the interesting part – together with my remembrance I received some kind of inner feeling, which helped me to understand and to decide which of my required elemental steps should be next for me to become a mature person. I actually don't like to call it 'inner feeling', but I really don't know how precisely to describe it. It happens occasionally and you can't not think about it; you can't just ignore that feeling. It was a feeling which helped me to understand my own transforming decisions.

Sometimes I could also feel it during conversations, work and other activities. So that was the reason why, after some time, I stopped writing my introspection status. From now on, I relied on this feeling and it never disappointed me. To describe this analogically, it felt like some small dwarf sitting on a barricade commanding me to do some precisely planned and required actions to crush that barricade. Sometimes he says nothing, because I need to endure a bit longer than expected to understand the reason behind it, like a Saturn teaching routine, being so happy with this feeling, to know when is the right time to bring the right decision. It made me think about it for a longer period of time, so I started to believe that it was a voice of Saturn or some Angel. Or at least, some higher energy that tried to give me a signal.

PART III: ESTABLISHING MAGICAL EQUILIBRIUM

After some time I got used to it; it became normal to me to do the self-transformation work without a pen and paper. I always followed my own inner feeling, which grew bigger over time. By each action, it felt as though I already knew everything. However, at that point I didn't assume that my old routine was unnecessary and useless. I was still well aware of it. But I pictured this feeling as a reward, a reward which helped me when I didn't have enough time or situation to write everything on paper and take care of my introspection notes.

Pretty soon my life challenged me again and I always said to myself. 'Yeah - Saturn is testing me again'. I thought maybe the feeling that I've overhauled myself with the trait removal plans was a reason for this. Then I realized that I focused my life too much on the whole trait transformation process, so much that I actually couldn't proceed further, no matter how hard I tried. To simplify this, I forgot to live my life normally. So I really had to stop doing the trait routine and paused the whole mirror process for some period of time. Fatigue and big life changes didn't give me enough chance to continue with it as before.

But I also didn't give up. I've tried to live further with it. This is the time when that feeling came in handy. I really envisioned this as an important part of transformation. Even if I did make some mistakes, it didn't made me feel stupid. It made me feel more emphatic to deeply understand that mistake and to realize why I actually needed to make that mistake – to learn something new and to be able to understand some unknown traits. We also know that everything takes its time – so does the learning process, realizing that we need to experience important parts of our life to proceed further with our transformation.

Let's say that Saturn put a wall in front of me. He doesn't want me to get rid of s particular trait before I learn something from this lacking life experience, but with this feeling everything makes sense to me. Understanding this blockade inspired me to immerse myself with future decisions and to break that wall.

This is the point where I really got used to this feeling and learned how to use it for my future transforming advantage, being astonished, to be able to understand each of my actions during unpredictable moments and to understand other people's reactions instantly. I couldn't get angry or dumbfounded anymore. I was able to understand my own behavior in certain situations and to act with my own will and to freely arrive at my own decisions, independent from other people around me. Receiving this kind of perspective is really mesmerising but at the same time it is a great way and a huge inspiration to continue your work in step 2 of IHH no matter the current life situation.

Taking too much time just to rearrange, count, research, correct and plan your mirror trait book over and over again can lead you to an obsession with no results, like some work projects that are just overplanned, too complicated and never saw the light of day, collecting dust somewhere on a shelf or nowadays on a hard drive.

Literally said: don't waste your time on too much planning – start living it. Look at each life situation as a challenge which rewards you with a new trait balance. Like some kind of life challenge hunter, start hunting your life chapters which could give you mirror trait achievement rewards, depending on your perspective and how you deal with them. Start living those introspection things that you write and investigate – you will understand them better and you may be faster in transforming those traits. However, I don't say you should stop writing and taking care of your trait notes. I'm just saying, don't preoccupy yourself with it.

That's my story and what I've learned during my transformation process. I was afraid of messing up my whole progress, but in the end I found out that it was possible to make transformations without pen and paper. This is not a trait elimination race, but a part of your own experience. You will understand your traits better and why you have them, and certainly find a perfect way to get rid of 'bad' ones. It will also be easier to do the 7-Pronged Attack when you understand your trait and the reason behind it during some activity and situation.

Let me tell just one of many anecdotes. I was not actually afraid of water but I felt some kind of shame and uncertainty because I couldn't swim anymore. At first I also thought that maybe I was just a bit too shy to show my body in front of others, because it goes in the same chain of personal reasons, but before the swimming problem, I had already found another trait and finally dealt with it.

During my childhood, my family was poor and we couldn't afford to go on a summer vacation. So I forgot how to swim and for my whole life I was avoiding going swimming in the sea or in a pool with my friends

PART III: ESTABLISHING MAGICAL EQUILIBRIUM

because I thought they will definitely laugh at me because I couldn't swim. Many hot summers I would rather stay at home instead of going with my friends to the public bathing place.

I had this in my trait list, but still it wasn't so easy, or fast enough, to do it with a 7-Pronged Attack. I already felt that it would require some deeper action. Not so long ago I admitted this to a dear friend of mine and he suddenly enrolled me to do the swimming course for adults. At first I was uncertain and I needed to take some time to think about it, but shortly after I accepted that and really went for it. One month later I had learned to swim and dive, like a fish, said the mentor. It was such a great experience to feel the movement and freedom in water for the first time after so many years. I couldn't describe this happiness.

A few months later I finally went for a holiday by the sea to swim and collect new experiences. With this my trait of bravery, shame and uncertainty has changed, simply just by living, being honest and accepting a life invitation.

Gounelle, in his book *The Man Who Wanted to Be Happy* wrote: 'Personally, I spend more time noticing what is wrong with my life than imagining an ideal life.' In this case we don't need to imagine an ideal life but just to live our life present-minded during the transformation process and everything will be much simpler.

After living and feeling the trait transformation more deeply with a bunch of new feelings, the next introspection will be deeper and will give you even better results. You will be rewarded with many other unexpected and beautiful things within yourself. You'll be happy to introspect yourself once again.

So don't worry if you currently don't have enough time for your progress. In that case, just try to feel, breathe and live in your transformation life opportunities.

4. Divine Purpose: Finding Your Why for Achieving Magical Equilibrium, Adepthood, and Beyond - Mahabija

Any serious and authentic magical tradition or spiritual cultivation method requires a serious attitude, discipline, commitment and an exceptional amount of will-power to succeed in any meaningful and measurable way. It's because of these requirements that so few actually succeed.

When you ask the average student why they have decided to take up the practice of their given magical tradition, the answer more times than not is some desire in the ego to perform magical feats comparable to what you might see in a blockbuster fantasy movie, where they can bend people to their will, manifest all their desires with a snap of a finger and ultimately become self-appointed masters of the world and the universe.

Rarely do the selfish desires of the ego, render the will, action, introspection and divine assistance necessary to help a student complete the rigorous path of obtaining magical equilibrium, adepthood and beyond.

> *'In other words, you have a slightly better chance of succeeding in your magical practice if you have a profound commitment from the beginning as to the way in which you wish to serve. Having inside knowledge – which magic gives – on how evolution and the universe work comes with very great responsibility. The divine world is much happier to assist you in your development if it senses you are already from day one aligned with its purposes.'*
>
> ~ William Mistele

The above quote is a response to a question I posed to the Magical Adept William Mistele, when I first discovered Franz Bardon's 'Initiation into Hermetics' and decided the Bardon tradition was the tradition and magical path I would undertake and dedicate myself to completing. To be honest I only had a vague understanding of what was being said and lacked the wisdom to clearly grasp the importance of this seed of wisdom. It was only much later that I would understand this idea and how eventually it would play a key role in my own journey.

The Master's Visit

As a student on the path, I claim no adepthood or even level of an initiate but can remember a past time, not too long ago, of struggle and frustration in my attempt to progress in the Bardon Tradition which has since left me.

This clarity came to me during a dream when a Magical Adept visited me along with my Holy Guardian Angel. During the dream an old man with a long gray beard appeared in front of me with a sword in hand as to challenge me in martial art combat. I moved toward him attempting to strike him with my own sword when in return he moved with lightning speed ending up behind me with his sword at my neck, 'You're dead'. I quickly tried to move and strike again only to find myself in the same position with his sword at my neck, 'You're dead again'. I quickly realized I was com-pletely at the mercy of this person and a huge amount of humility swept over me. At that moment I realized how little I knew, as the combat rep-resented my level of knowledge and wisdom in comparison to his own.

The Master then made it known that he would take me under his tutelage but only after I had mastered what he called *'The Basics'*. He stated that I must embody the qualities of the Gnome and approach my practice step by step, building *'Brick by Brick'* without ever ceasing. Only then would I have the stable foundation necessary to progress further and transition into the higher teachings and practices of spiritual cultivation.

After waking from this dream, I was gifted with inspiration and a newfound commitment toward my practices. First, I knew that I was not alone on my journey and secondly, that I would never cease in my practice no matter what. I also discovered a new joy in practicing and developing each skill, even if it took a lifetime. My focus and joy was now in the process and no longer in the end result.

EQUIPOISE: INSIGHTS INTO FOUNDATIONAL ASTRAL TRAINING

A few days passed and I began to contemplate the experience again. I began to wonder why this Master visited me in the first place. I then remembered the words of William Mistele.

The divine world is much happier to assist you in your development if it senses you are already from day one aligned with its purposes.

Although I was indeed struggling with my spiritual cultivation, my heartfelt intent has always been aligned with what might be called 'Divine Purpose'. Intuitively I feel this was the reason for my visitation and divine assistance, along with the reaching of a certain level of maturity.

Finding Your Why

A good number of men and women possess a desire to undertake the training of a magical or spiritual cultivation tradition. But the reason or 'Why' they want to do it when contemplated, will reveal a great deal about themselves, their desires, weaknesses and if they have reached a level of maturity that could potentially lead them into alignment with a more meaningful life purpose and more successful spiritual cultivation practice.

There are countless amounts of techniques and methods amongst magical traditions and spiritual cultivation schools. In the Bardon tradition, there are many tools and methods described to assist a student on the path to achieve elemental equilibrium. In Virgil's book *The Elemental Equilibrium* he goes into great detail discussing the 'six-pronged attack' which is a collection of methods from the Bardon tradition that can assist an individual in obtaining elemental equilibrium – Auto-suggestion, Volition, Conscious Eating, Conscious Breathing, Magical Washing, and Trans-mutation.

In Ray del Sole's *Preliminary Practice for Franz Bardon's Initiation into Hermetics*, he states the importance of strengthening one's will-power through mental exercises of concentration on the Ajna chakra. According to Ray, the Ajna chakra is the master chakra and center of will, mental fire element, and focused consciousness.

For some, the tools and strategies provided by Magical Adepts which have come before in their tradition may be all that is needed to successfully progress along the path. For many more, it will most likely be a struggle but I believe that struggle can be lessened by aligning one's intent with a Divine Purpose.

William Mistele has graciously provided a list of Divine Missions that students can undertake as their own Life Purpose or simply inspire them to create their own Divine Mission.

> Create a new religion
> Establish a Spiritual Community
> Become a Guardian Angel
> Master of Magical Silence
> Magical Therapy
> Magical Healer
> The Feminine Mysteries, Part II
> Teach the Mysteries to the Masses
> Troubadour of Divine Providence
> Global Prophet at Large
> Master of the Elements
> Agent of Divine Providence
> Uncover the Mystery Unfolding in Another's Life
> Guardian ad Litem for Atlantis
> Guardian of the Gate to the Realm of Undines

Committing to a Life Purpose that is inspired by the Divine will not only help you gain the assistance of Divine Providence but will also assist you in your own daily motivation and provide a more stable journey lit by a pathway of humility and compassion allowing you to avoid many of the trappings and pitfalls of the Ego.

Divine Vows

In the Buddhist tradition, a Bodhisattva is a person who has undertaken the path to obtain Buddhahood for the benefit of all sentient beings. In this pursuit, he takes a vow to achieve a variety of levels of spiritual perfection in an effort to assist all sentient beings in all kinds of different matters.

The Bodhisattva, Quan Yin, vowed to stay in the earthly realms without ascending until all other living beings completed their own enlightenment and freed themselves of the cycle of samsara. There are many other devas who have made similar vows and become Bodhisattvas.

Because it takes so much time, discipline and commitment to achieve magical equilibrium, adepthood and beyond, it's important to ask yourself why you want to spend so much time dedicating yourself to achieving these states.

The next question you might want to ask yourself is, once you achieve these states and all the responsibilities that go with it, what will you do with it? Will you utilize your wisdom and abilities to make the lives of your family, friends or humanity more fulfilling? There is no right answer to these questions but since your motivation will play a big part in whether you succeed or not, it seems that this is something every student on the path should begin to question and answer as soon as they can.

Developing your own personal Divine Vow or Oath and repeating it daily is a powerful way to strengthen and commit your mind, body and spirit with your intentions. If those intentions are heartfelt and truly aligned with the divine, your chances of succeeding in your chosen magical or spiritual tradition will be that much greater since your will is aligned with the will of the Divine World.

Life Regret Minimization

Jeff Bezos, the founder of Amazon.com, coined the phrase 'Life Regret Minimization'. The idea is that you project yourself into the future to around the age of eighty or so and look back at any potential regrets you might have in an attempt to make better decisions in your life, so that you avoid experiencing those regrets.

This is a really powerful framework that can also be applied to spiritual cultivation. If you were truly serious about progressing in your chosen magical tradition and were to continue doing the same things that you are doing now up until the age of eighty, would you have any regrets? Would you have accomplished everything that you wanted to accomplish and which deep down you knew you were capable of?

PART III: ESTABLISHING MAGICAL EQUILIBRIUM

Projecting into the future and imagining your ideal self, what qualities and characteristics would you possess? What impact have you had on the world, your friends and your family? Getting clear on who that person is, is a great way to align and potentially find your Life Purpose. And when that Purpose is aligned with Divine, miracles can indeed happen!

Conclusion

In Franz Bardon's second book, 'The Practice of Magical Evocation', he describes 360 intelligences of the Zone Girdling the Earth. Each one of these intelligences possesses an infinite amount of wisdom and knowledge pertaining to all kinds of affairs on Earth. Any one of them could provide the inspiration and the lifelong tutelage of their specific expertise to be learned and expressed in the world for the betterment of all life and civilization.

The discovery of one's Life Purpose is a journey in itself but the first step starts with simply contemplating your own reasons for wanting to take up your given magical or spiritual tradition. Success has a great deal to do with reaching a certain level of maturity and beginning to ask yourself why you want to commit to a lifelong journey of magical and spiritual cultivation which will begin to set the stage to discovering your own Divine Purpose.

5. How to Deal with Emotional Resistance – Gabriel Moreira

Probably at some point in time you already experienced a sudden sensation of being tired, indisposed, sleepy, worn-out, restless, a sensation of aversion, in the moment you decided to study something important, to do some domestic duty, meditation, physical exercises, talk to someone, or even take a break to breath.

And also the opposite: to feel suddenly cheered up at the moment you received some good news, a gift, when talking about something interesting, meeting a specific person and so on.

Many times it goes beyond our physical state, how much we rested that day, if we eat well; and this sensation can manifest specially when we are trying to build a new habit, or to adjust an old one, anything that takes us away of the familiar, of our current routine, even if a part of us really wants to change.

We can call that 'Emotional Resistance'.

Here are four possible approaches I found to deal with this, based on the four Elements.

1. Maybe you like challenges. To meet an internal resistance can create a stimulus for you to persist, a motivation to expand your own limitations. If you are a creative person, you can transform something initially boring into a very entertaining activity.
2. You can be more neutral. Observing the resistance with detachment, something that is what it is, without considering it as a problem or something to worry about. Just accept it, pay attention to what it can tell you.
3. It is possible to create an internal dialogue for transforming things from inside out. Maybe this resistance wants to show you something that was ignored, a genuine need that could not be satisfied. Talk to it. Forgive yourself, accept, shelter yourself; pay attention to the parts of you that are wounded,

PART III: ESTABLISHING MAGICAL EQUILIBRIUM

afraid, or not recognised and tell them that you love them. Tell them why what you want to do is good for your being as a whole. Invite all parts of yourself to work together.
4. You can focus in the awareness of the physical body, in the sensations. Watch, be open to perceptions, observe your state of presence, seek to understand objectvely all that you are feeling – including the discomforts and resistances which can be located in an specific body area. Work with patience and constancy, respecting, and relating to, your own physical and emotional limits.

Naturally, we can combine more than one option and/or find different approaches.

It may also be productive, in some cases, to try a more distant approach to your personality.

Which one(s) do you like most?

6. Establishing Magical Equilibrium – A Miscellany of Information – Christian Lindo Ntanzi

Conscious Eating Tips

Conscious eating had a strong impact on my life when I was growing up. I did it without knowing its effects but they materialized greatly.

I was raised Christian and I took every step of my progress seriously and one of them was taking Holy Communion. I think when we were told about Holy Communion my imagination about it kick-started my great experiences. My experience after conscious taking of Holy Communion was a shock when I realized that I would not go hungry for the whole day and I felt somehow really strong.

Seemingly all sorts of worldly things seemed gloomy, because I would become ecstatic or tranquil. I carried on with the same thing when I began with *Initiation into Hermetics*. My tip is, before you do any sort of conscious eating, first make sure you are clean in terms of the soul mirrors. We used to call it forgiveness of past transgressions and then be ready to be united with Christ consciousness in the form of Holy Communion. Completely dissolve yourself into the thing you want to achieve, as if you can feel it already while you are imagining and impregnating your desire in your food. Make it simple and work with one desire at a time.

I found out that lifelong desires like character shaping are the best and have a good success rate because your mind is not triggered into hastiness and impatience for the outcome since you are patient and you learn quickly when you persevere with one thing until it happens. Magic seems to yield more for unselfish desires and it seems to know your true intentions like when you need health, so I encourage you to begin with simple and moralistic desires like health or inner strengths.

PART III: ESTABLISHING MAGICAL EQUILIBRIUM

Conscious Breathing Tips

With conscious breathing, I would say our minds go haywire sometimes and we even forget to breath calmly. I discovered this when I was very frustrated and one of my friends introduced a shocking trick to me that I was not aware of. As I explained my trouble to him he gave a moment of silence as if he was on to something trying to find a solution to my complaint. He asked me to relax a bit and showed me how much I was blowing my energy – my body was even stiff as if I was ready to run or fight. I came into my presence, my shoulders were high and stiff. He asked me to bring them lower and to release my hands and relax. After that he asked me not to think of anything and draw my breath in and out .It was an amazing feeling. I felt so relieved – tension was releasing and energy was coming back. Breathing was so good that I didn't realize something that I missed out previouly – I had been breathing without awareness.

My tip would be to relax and sit in a quiet space and be still; all thoughts have to be eliminated because thought draws and depletes energy. Early morning breathing is best because your mind is clean, still open for suggestions and morning air is fresh. When I do breathing in a clean quiet space, afterwards I always feel as though I have taken a bath because of the vitality I receive from impregnating air with a fresh mind.

Auto-suggestion Tips

I always use repetition – every chance I get to implant a wish I repeat, repeat and repeat, until my inner voice says it without my conscious mind being too aware of it. Auto-suggestion requires a state of mind where you are very tranquil or in a light mood – your mind is not buzzing with too many thoughts. I have used my subconscious mind facing big challenges. How many things have we said to ourselves when checked with temporary defeat only to see them manifesting again and again and wondering how? But when facing challenging emotions I try to say that this is not my true self – I am a well-mannered and happy person and speak the opposite situation of what I am challenged. I say this because when we are emotional, a great deal of the subconscious mind is involved, so why not take the opportunity to transmute bad experiences into positive ones?

Anecdotes regarding the step 2 self-transformation work

I can say that auto-suggestion works so much better when the desire is not too selfish or involves negative values. But I have used it in a desperate moment when my employment at that time was taking a toll of my health. It meant that I needed to change from one workshop to a different one. The workshop was just a couple of blocks from where I was working. I went to ask for an available post with determination and the manager was pleased to see someone determined to be looking for the vacant position. However if I wanted it, it had to be authorized through a chain of command.

I was involved with a group that was devoted to praying. We had a huge mat made of sack material that was charged like a magic circle and when you step on it you are activating power so you can manifest. My method was to prepare myself by a form of washing my sins first, then focusing on my intent and activating my subconscious mind. I would lose my self entirely and be in a form of ecstasy, then I would plant my desire to get the new position. I repeated this method because it was a good space to work with my subconscious mind. I felt that I was already occupying this position and I had no worry or doubtful thoughts. It was something that happened on its own and it didn't take very long while continuing to ask about my application. I was taken on the post.

About the psychic training experience, when I began to feel a physical change in the brain and movement inside, it was first a soft tingling feeling above my skull and as I continued after visualization of the object, I felt heat. It felt as though the more I felt heat, the more things seemed to be taking shape, because whenever I did a successful ritual or some sort of intense prayer with visualization, my brain felt hot.

General tips and advice regarding self transformation work

A student must take all exercises seriously. A student must always have a will to succeed and know that sometimes the results may not be instant, so patience and devotion are required. Auto-suggestion works very well with true unselfish desires, so dealing with soul mirrors will help a lot because negative character and values drag you back. With auto-suggestion,

PART III: ESTABLISHING MAGICAL EQUILIBRIUM

if you're confident with what you want, you will worry less about it and yet still be very determined – the feelings will be as though you already have affinity with what you desire, as if you already possess it and there is no over confidence. Stay away from thoughts, things that deplete your will-power, that are draining energy. You might be required to change your environment, or you can use it to help you strengthen your magic by transmuting challenges of your environment to make you a strong person.

Mistakes made during the step 2 astral work and what you learned from those mistakes

With auto-suggestion I wanted to achieve big goals first. This is not wise. I learned that gratitude helps you forward – you learn the importance and power of small things first, then more will come and it will be easier to achieve. I wanted quick results in the beginning, but I learned that quick results have no lessons and usually demoralize you if they do not show up in time.

Due to excitement I thought more of myself in comparison to others who don't practice magic so I learnt that you 'don't walk with your halo', – don't boast or let the world know your magical achievements or exercise it unnecessarily – it's immature.

While doing physical training in the asana position I lost consciousness and passed out due to the difficult position I took. I learned that some positions are for the experienced or you might seek guidance so that you won't do what you don't know and risk danger and injury.

7. The Six-Pronged Attack – Ilyas Rahhali

Elemental equilibrium is such an important topic in Bardon's system, but is often the exercise most neglected by practitioners. Perhaps the reason for this is that the beginner students of magic do not see its value and are looking to perform 'magic'. However, they could not be more wrong, if for no other reason that one should take this exercise seriously for one's own safety. Bardon warns many times against practicing elemental exercises without making progress in the elemental equilibrium part of one's development.

Moreover, in my opinion, it is the best exercise in the first two steps of *Initiation into Hermetics* and offers practical, tangible, real-life results. It requires patience, will-power and self-compassion to introspectively and objectively sort out one's layers of character traits – these exercises hold tremendous benefits. You can basically change your whole personality if you wish to and get rid of traits that are holding you back in your life.

I have found that the six-pronged attack[3] is the best tool to achieve that, because it it is not only the most effective technique, but also puts you in a positive feedback loop where the techniques work exponentially faster and better the more results you get with them and the stronger you believe in them.

The Six-Pronged Attack is listed below:

1. Auto-suggestion

2. Volition

3. Conscious eating

4. Conscious breathing

5. Magical washing

---

3   The Six-Pronged Attack is referenced from *The Elemental Equilibrium* by Virgil pp 6-7

PART III: ESTABLISHING MAGICAL EQUILIBRIUM

6. Transmutation

To illustrate how powerful these techniques are, let me tell you a little story. Four years ago, I got into the habit of sleeping really late, at least at two a.m. every day. I 'snoozed' the alarm clock at least five times, even though I put the phone away, or set it to solve mathematical problems before the alarm went off. I was just solving them, snoozing and going back to sleep half consciously. It was my new norm and habit. As I started working the Bardon system, I always wanted to start waking up at five a.m. to do the exercises in the morning. But since another of my biggest flaws is that I found it extremely hard to stick to new habits, I couldn't push through from using sheer will alone, however strong my will was. I had been annoyed and frustrated about it for a long time and sometimes hated myself for not being able to wake up early.

Recently, I decided to apply the six-pronged attack to this trait and hoped to transform it. At the time, I was still skeptical about it working for me, telling myself that I was different from those for whom it had worked and that even if it worked for other people, it might not work for me, especially since it hadn't worked much for my desire to acquire the ability to dream lucidly. Since I was so desperate to change that habit, I told myself I had nothing to lose going all out, but I had everything to win.

So I picked up again Virgil's *Elemental Equilibrium* book, quickly looked again for advice on applying the six-pronged attack, and applied it during the day with as much conviction as I was capable of.

For every meal and drink I had, I focused and tried, firmly believing that I was eating the quality of waking up early. Every time I washed my hands that day and during my shower, I focused on the water absorbing my laziness and resistance to waking up and taking it down the sinkhole, away from me. On my bike ride that day, I kept repeating to myself out loud the suggestion that I can easily wake up early full of energy and alertness.

The next morning, I was so shocked and surprised that I woke up before my alarm went off, and also I was surprisingly alert and aware without the irresistible reflex of snoozing again. It was a huge difference from my normal mornings where I was half conscious, moving on reflexes and my mind shutting down. My faith in the process has skyrocketed since that day. I started the soul mirror exercise again with more care, seriousness and discipline, this time after witnessing the power of the techniques. Old character traits that were limiting me since my teens and which I wished didn't have, seemed easier to get rid of now, while some very desirable traits I wished I was born with started looking pleasantly within reach.

Let's explore the story of Raymond and Claudia. Both are practitioners of Bardon's system and are in the third step of IIH. After some time practicing elemental pore breathing, both were confronted with a similar situation. Raymond got into an argument with his partner, while Claudia was discussing with her friend and at some point they got opposite opinions on a subject, each defending his own. Raymond felt anger brewing inside. He started shouting and said some very mean things to his partner who, sobbing, went to lock herself in her room. Claudia felt anger growing in her as well. She then immediately started breathing anger out and breathing patience in for a few seconds. She also excused herself and went to the bathroom and flushed out anger through cold water. She then came back to her friend, and told her that they should just agree to disagree on that topic and that it would be best to change the topic.

When Raymond saw his significant other sobbing, and found himself alone in the room, he instantly felt bad about his behavior and regretted it. He didn't know why he reacted that way because it wasn't in his nature to act on anger. He sometimes felt irritated and felt some anger, but he could always contain it and control it. The thing he hadn't realized was that when he started reading the third step of IIH, he paid little attention to the warnings the chapter started with. He also skipped the soul mirror exercise, and for the purification of character exercise in the second step of IIH, he just put random self-help subliminal messages into the music he often listened to.

This story illustrates how dangerous an imbalanced progression through the stages is and especially the soul mirror exercises. If you don't do the mastery of the mind exercises well, it's relatively safe to skip exercises ahead, because then you don't have enough mental power and control to do the elemental exercises correctly and as such they have no effect and are harmful. But when you skip the elemental equilibrium ones, you start getting effects like Raymond started noticing in himself. Your negative traits become amplified by the elemental energies you start working with, starting from the third step. While he could hold and control his anger previously, when he started the elemental pore breathing exercises, the anger became amplified

PART III: ESTABLISHING MAGICAL EQUILIBRIUM

and he was surprised at how it overwhelmed him. Let us hope that Raymond learns his lesson and goes back to doing his purification of the soul exercises well before starting to work again on the third step.

Claudia on the other hand, having scrupulously followed the balanced order of the exercises and having heeded the warning Bardon put before the third step, had rooted out the most problematic traits in her character and had kept in check others, so that she attended to them whenever they arose. She had no difficulty noticing the anger arising, and immediately used some of the fast working prongs to get rid of it mo-mentarily until it's this trait's turn to be slain by the mighty power of the six-pronged attack. With this mature behavior and approach to her training, she can safely progress through IIH. And for her, what had been a danger and a trap for Raymond, is a blessing for her. That is because working with elemental energies boosts all the character traits of a person, be they positive or negative. But since she's purifying herself more and more, the negative ones become weaker and weaker under the six pronged attack, while the positive ones become stronger and shinier through elemental pore breathing.

8. How do I Control my Subconscious Mind? - Tanya Robinson

"Until you make the unconscious conscious, it will direct your life and you will call it fate."

—C.G. Jung

"There is this one green lion, which closes and opens the seven indissoluble seals of the seven metallic spirits which torments the bodies, until it has perfected them, by means of the artist's long and resolute patience." — "The Cosmopolite," (16th century).

'*The Green Lion Devouring The Sun*' is a popular alchemical symbol. On a chemical level this is a metaphor for when a green, liquid sulfate called "vitriol" purifies matter, leaving behind the gold within the matter. Very pure vitriol is an acid that eats through practically anything, except gold.

The internal alchemical process of transformation has often been symbolised with the green lion eating the sun, which later becomes transformed into red by the sun. The green is symbolic of the *materia prima* (the grossest form of matter in its chaotic form) and in alchemical terms it is a green liquid of sulfate called "virtriol". Vitriol is an acid that will eat through the grossest of substances except gold. We can see the metaphor in the above image as the symbol of the destructive tormentors of the body being acted out, represented by the lion devouring the sun.

On a human level, the green lion eating the sun is a metaphor for when a person's *"consciousness [is] overwhelmed by violent, frustrated desires"* (Fabricus).

PART III: ESTABLISHING MAGICAL EQUILIBRIUM

In the *Corpus Hermeticum XIII Hermes*[4] speaking to his 'son' Tat these tormentors are revealed,

> *Her.* Torment the first is this Not-knowing, 1 son; the second one is Grief; the third, Intemperance; the fourth, Concupiscence; the fifth, Unrighteousness; the sixth is Avarice; the seventh, Error 2; the eighth is Envy; the ninth, Guile 3; the tenth is Anger; eleventh, Rashness; the twelfth is Malice. These are in number twelve; but under them are many more, my son; and creeping through the prison of the body 4 they force the man that's placed within 5 to suffer in his senses. But they depart (although not all at once) from him who hath been taken pity on by God 6; and this it is which constitutes the manner of Rebirth. And . . . . 7 the Reason (*Logos*). 8. And now, my son, be still and solemn silence keep! Thus shall the mercy that flows on us from God not cease. Henceforth rejoice, O son, for by the Powers of God thou art being purified for the articulation of the Reason (*Logos*).

In modern day language I believe Hermes was referring to the uncontrolled or hidden aspect of the subconscious mind that refers to the negative expression of qualities — the tormentors which he lists twelve. Interestingly, Hermes also speaks about a solution to dealing with these forces and offers a key, the use of the *logos* (reasoning), which I believe is referring to the conscious aspect of the mind. Later on in this article we will see how not only this sentence of knowledge is fundamental in transforming the mind, but also the importance of using the *logos* to practice conscious awareness in daily life; moreover, we should understand the influence that the subconscious mind has upon us. Also, we will be delving into the nature of concentration, its importance and link to the subconscious mind, including how the ability to make progress in any path towards adepthood is linked to the ability to concentrate and control our thoughts.

4Mead G.R.S. *Corpus Hermeticum* XIII. (XIV.)*Thrice-Greatest Hermes – Volume 2.*

What is the conscious and subconscious mind and why are they so important in our hermetic training?

You will have probably come across this dealing with this aspect of the mind through any self-development program, or through working on auto-suggestion if you follow the Bardon system. In modern psychology the subconscious aspect of the mind refers to a vast collection of unintentional, habitual thoughts, behaviors, and actions. These actions are non-conscious which in fact means we have no choice in the way the mind responds.

The iceberg model for conscious and subconscious mind

Neuroscientists[5] have come to the understanding that the brain's processes operate much like the metaphor of an iceberg, whereby 10% of the conscious mind is active and in our control and 90% is hidden and is controlled by the subconscious aspect of the mind's processes. In earlier an text, Hermes makes reference to uncontrolled passions relating to the tormentors. I believe he is referring to the negative uncontrolled aspect of the subconscious mind.

If we look at the list below which attributes are associated with the uncontrolled subconscious mind it is very interesting to note the form of these tormentors often manifest through them.

- Beliefs
- Emotions
- Habits
- Values
- Protective reactions
- Long-term memory
- Imagination
- Intuition

Most people are subject to dealing with negative experiences from the past. Emotions rising up through protective reactions, or people believing they are cursed. Bad habits preventing them from having a full expression in

---

5   http://journalpsyche.org/understanding-the-human-mind/

life. The cultural values imposed upon us through our upbringing, to name a few.

Now let us look at the conscious mind in which only 10% of is conscious, meaning thoughts and actions that we actively choose through our own will (as illustrated in the iceberg metaphor). If we go back to the references to Hermes he speaks about the *logos* in terms of logical reasoning, and if we look at the attributes below associated with the conscious mind we can see there is a direct link.

- Will-power
- Short-term memory
- Logical thinking
- Critical thinking

This again is very interesting. If you look at any training that focuses on adepthood you will note at that will-power, logical thinking, and critical thinking are key to having clarity of mind and to overriding the subconscious processes. As you can see, working on the mind is paramount if we wish to succeed. We have a huge challenge ahead of us since 90% of our mind is not our own.

Not only are we dealing with this fact but we are increasingly faced with the challenges of modern day society, where we are constantly experiencing so much stimulation around us. Our level of ability for concentrating on one thing at one time has greatly diminished as we have become more accustomed to multitasking. It is such a great issue now that we even have a medical term for it: attention-deficit/hyperactivity disorder (ADHD).

A study performed by Microsoft 2015[6] studied the brain activity of 2,000 Canadian subjects researching the brain wave activity of concentration levels using an electroencephalogram. The conclusion from the experiment showed that the average attention span dropped from 12 seconds in a study in 2000 to eight seconds in 2013.

---

6 Microsoft Attention Spans, 2015.

One conclusion the study pointed out was that our ability to multitask has drastically improved in the mobile age, however the ability to concentrate showed a correlation between users':

1. Volume of media consumption
2. Social media usage
3. Multi-Screening behaviour
4. Adoption of technology

The study concluded that "digital lifestyles affect the ability to remain focused for long periods of time," suggesting that our subconscious mind is running the show and our conscious decision making has vastly reduced.

A number of online sites suggest the conclusion that attention spans are decreasing in time: Attention spans have shrunk by 50 percent over the past decade. Children diagnosed with ADHD: .

Not only are we having to deal with a media-driven environment that is continually bombarding us with stimulation, all this information is also being absorbed by the subconscious. Our minds are being overloaded with information continuously, which is a contributing a factor that affects our ability to concentrate. We have established that 90% of our thoughts and actions are not conscious. We can now see the importance of being careful in what we expose ourselves to on a daily basis. What we watch and read, what we engage in, is continuously being processed by the subconscious mind including past experiences, actions, thoughts and feelings.

Now let us take a look at subconscious mind from a hermetic viewpoint.

The hermetic view of the subconscious mind

Franz Bardon[7] describes the subconscious as;

The subconscious is the mirror to all negative attributes and is located in the inter-brain in the astral body. The uncontrolled

---

7 Rüggeberg D, Franz Bardon *Questions and Answers and the Great Arcanum, Compiled from teachings of Franz Bardon,* Merkur Publishing, Inc,2009.

PART III: ESTABLISHING MAGICAL EQUILIBRIUM

subconscious is our enemy. It is especially effective at night, in space without time, in the body when the normal consciousness is at rest.

How do I deal with the subconscious mind?

I have offered 3 different approaches from Franz Bardon, Martin Faulks and Virgil.

In Step II of Bardon's *Initiation into Hermetics*[8], he offers a comprehensive chapter discussing subconscious and how to overcome it through using tools such as autosuggestion, and using the magnetic forces to impregnate positive influences using methods such as magical washing and, magical eating. He also offers advice in *Questions and Answers* as follows,

We can control our subconscious through autosuggestion if we order it to do something good for us just before we fall asleep. We assign the subconscious to our storehouse of ideas where it exists as our qualitative component. Its quantity is the power to effect and tension of the opposite negative attributes.

Here Bardon is offering us a key by transmuting the qualitative component of negative thoughts to positive ones, and by using the quantity of our will-power and volition to bring about change.

We can see also Martin Faulks takes a similar approach whereby he tackles this aspect of the subconscious by making positive conscious choices and behaviours in daily life, which over time become habitual. This approach not only takes control by using the conscious mind, but also changes the negative patterns of the subconscious mind to positive ones. In Enlightened Living[9] he discusses using this is approach, not only its effectiveness, but also how it can lead to a permanent state of higher awareness:

---

8 Bardon, F, *Initiation Into Hermetics*, (Step II Autosuggestion or the Secret of the Subconscious), Merkur Publishing, Inc. 10th ed, 2107.

9 Faulks M, *Enlightened Living, Chapter 5, (The Greatest Barrier to Enlightenment)*2nd ed, Falcon Books Publishing, 2009.

So the idea is to make this state of consciousness our normal functioning state of consciousness. To do this, it is very important to learn to fully engage in what is happening right now. To always remember that the enlightened person is not going to be beyond troubles, but is rather someone who skilfully deals to the best of his or her ability, with the goal to bring about the best possible outcome. So when a negative thought enters the mind, it is corrected and then transformed into something positive. Rather than assuming failure at the presence of a negative thought, it is important to correct the mind. It is unrealistic to expect to never have those kinds of thoughts. Indeed to me, this very act of transforming a negative action or thought into something that has positive intentions and outcomes embodies the highest expression of enlightenment.

Using this method, not only does the individual begin to train the conscious mind by being in the present moment, but they also bring into awareness the uncontrolled negative aspects of the subconscious, which are then brought into line by being corrected immediately as they arise. He further offers some motivating affirmations and finally states,

The importance of applying these skills in our waking day cannot be emphasised enough. In spiritual traditions this is endemic. As people continually search for new techniques upon new techniques but never realising that these techniques are only the training, it is the embodiment of the skills, insights and abilities that aid us in daily life.

To review:

1. Do not put this off.
2. It will not suddenly happen.
3. Spiritual exercises are training, the true test is applying the lessons to life.
4. Embody the state you wish to happen.
5. Own every single action.

PART III: ESTABLISHING MAGICAL EQUILIBRIUM

By applying these principles, balance will be found within ourselves because by practicing things that are difficult we become stronger in those areas we are weakest. This acts as a sunlamp on the soul. Skills are transferable, so as we become accomplished in one particular skill, our ability improves in other areas also. For me, this is the true way of enlightenment.

Virgil in *The Elemental* Equilibrium[10] again takes the step 2 approach of Bardon's three-pronged attack, of using autosuggestion, transmutation and volition, and adds a further 3 to the mix, which he calls the "six-pronged attack." He states,

> *Autosuggestion, volition, conscious eating, conscious breathing and magical washing are specific techniques you can use to transform yourself. Transmutation is not a specific technique, but a strategy. The idea to eliminate a negative trait by developing the opposite trait. For example if you want to eliminate impatience from your personality you can do this by developing patience.*

In this method Virgil is tackling directly the subconscious by continually using a focused approach by charging up the food and, the breath, and when washing to aid in transforming negative qualities.

Concentration linked to the subconscious mind

Our ability to concentrate is fundamental in any spiritual discipline if we wish to progress to any degree.

Why is this so?

Because we need to have conscious awareness over our thoughts and actions in order to know that these processes are actually from our own choice and not through a programmed response generated by our

---

10 Virgil, *The Elemental Equilibrium: Notes on the Foundation of Magical Adepthood,* Falcon Books Publishing, 2017

subconscious mind. In order for us to enter into deep concentration we need to clear the underlying vibration or noise that is preventing us from entering into a deep state of uninterrupted relaxation.

> *During concentration there is a continuity of consciousness and this condition allows our subconscious forces to rise up. The hidden psychological patterns in the subconscious mind start to manifest. Normally, because of our mental distractions, we are totally unable to contact or express our inner power. During deep periods of concentration we start to understand the deeper aspects of our being. So the fruits of concentration are substantial. Many people, whether they have experienced meditation or not, know that great things are in store for them if*
>
> *only they can concentrate deeply. Because they are not relaxed, however, they force their consciousness to dwell on one point.*[11]
>
> – Swami Satyananda Saraswati

As we can understand by this quote, our ability to concentrate is linked to a level of relaxation, a deep level of relaxation directly linked to the relationship we have with our subconscious mind. As Bardon states, often it is the uncontrolled subconscious mind that will bring up negative thoughts and fears generating an underlying anxiety within us. This often manifests in our dreams and when we are in a resting state.

Within the Franz Bardon training system in *Initiation Into Hermetics* in the first step Bardon addresses the power of the subconscious mind and how best to utilise it to our advantage, offering a number of tools to assist. However, this is a continual process throughout life as we continually refine the process of the inner alchemy of turning metal into gold.

---

[11] Swami Satyananda Saraswati, *A Systematic Course in the Ancient Tantric Techniques of Yoga and Kriya,* Yoga Publications Trust, Munger, Bihar, India, 2004.

PART III: ESTABLISHING MAGICAL EQUILIBRIUM

Why is it so important to have the ability to concentrate for spiritual development?

Within the many traditional spiritual traditions a lot of focus is placed on developing a high degree of concentration.

If you notice Bardon's focus is all on developing quantities and qualities in order to push through the realm of the mundane through use concentration to develop imagination skills and willpower. In traditional yoga the process of transformation of the soul follows a similar path. If you go back to our iceberg model you will also notice that all these qualities are in fact created by the conscious mind-the 10% that is visible to us. The ability to concentrate and use our will shows that we are have the ability to act in awareness and not to be guided by our subconscious mind. This is fundamental in training. You will notice Bardon also places importance on autosuggestion, magical washing, eating and drinking. Now we can begin to see why. He is aware of the power of the subconscious mind and has put everything in place to combat it.

What is concentration?

Franz Bardon describes concentration in *Questions and Answers*[12], taken from the yogic tradition as:

> "*Concentration* is an uninterrupted hold or adherence to a point, matter, being, abstract, concept, picture, thought, perception etc. Concentration is divided into three levels according with the periods of time. The first level is uninterrupted concentration for twelve seconds is called *dharana*. The second level is *dhyana*, has a duration of twelve times twelve seconds, while the third level has a duration of twelve times twelve times twelve seconds and this is called *samadhi* which means ecstasy, the flowing together of object and subject."

---

12 Rüggeberg D, Franz Bardon *Questions and Answers and the Great Arcanum, Compiled from teachings of Franz Bardon*, Merkur Publishing, Inc,2009.

Another quote by from a yogic perspective.[13]

Concentration implies the focusing of one's consciousness towards one point, either external or internal, to the exclusion of all other subjects or thoughts

. – Swami Satyananda Saraswati

What does this mean?

Through developing our concentration it allows us to not only gain a deeper knowledge of a subject with clarity and precision but also to merge with it. To penetrate the visible world and go beyond what is in front of us. When dealing with unseen forces it is paramount that we perceive through clarity and free from the bias of the subconscious mind. Only through willfully acting is this possible. But I believe the author is also talking about entering into a deep relaxation free from the noise of the subconscious mind.

So far we have established the power of the subconscious mind and how little our conscious mind takes part in daily life. We can also see the effects of our environment upon the conscious mind as our ability to act consciously diminishes due to the constant stimulation around us. Another converse effect is our ability to concentrate. So it is not surprising that people following the path of adepthood are faced with an even greater challenge than their predecessors. We need even a greater discipline to avoid daily distractions.

Why does my mind keep wandering when trying to concentrate on visualization?

Concentrating on one thing is a challenge for the mind because of the wandering tendency of the consciousness. It takes time for the body and mind to relax. In order to really concentrate we need to allow time for this to occur. Due to having busy lifestyles and distractions, most of us are not able to spend the length of time in covering all the aspects needed to really allow time for the parasympathetic nervous system to take effect and to sink into

---

13 Swami Satyananda Saraswati, *A Systematic Course in the Ancient Tantric Techniques of Yoga and Kriya*, Yoga Publications Trust, Munger, Bihar, India, 2004.

these practices. The passage below eloquently offers an explanation from a yoga perspective:

> *Many systems of yoga tell you to place an object in front of you or to visualize an internal image, concentrate on it, and lo and behold you will start to explore the subconscious depths of the mind. Although the method is correct and can bring wonderful experiences, it takes no consideration of the wandering tendency of our consciousness, which makes concentration impossible for most people. Concentration is possible only if a person is very relaxed mentally and physically. Most people cannot relax, or if they do it is on rare occasions. For this reason the mind continually projects streams of differing thoughts to conscious perception. As such, to ask most people to concentrate is impossible. And if they try to concentrate, they will tend to try to suppress the disturbing factors in the mind and create more tension in themselves.........Concentration is something that occurs spontaneously in a very relaxed mind and body. Until relaxation is achieved, concentration, real concentration that is, remains impossible. A system is required which progressively leads a person to deeper states of relaxation, until concentration becomes the spontaneous activity of consciousness.[8]*
>
> *– Swami Satyananda Saraswati*

Why can't I stop my thoughts in meditation?

I wanted to address how one of the main sticking points in any initiation that one will come across in meditation is being able to meditate with the cessation of thoughts. Many practitioners have this problem. As previously stated, the mind has a tendency to go into and follow a stream of consciousness. Unless we begin to address this in our daily life we are only scratching the surface. I believe the lack of concentration in daily life may be a contributing factor and the fact we are not able to enter a deep level of relaxation because we are not allowing enough time for the subconscious mind to process and release the tension that it has created.

If you look around you most people are constantly on their phones in daily life. We are feeding the subconscious continually. If mediation practice is one hour a day but the rest of the time at work or at home is being run by the subconscious mind, then when we sit in our meditation it is no wonder our subconscious mind will be processing thoughts. In effect we are training our subconscious mind, not our conscious mind. We all live such busy lives and the mind and body never really experience a state of relaxation. Learning to become aware of the mental processes throughout the day and cutting negative thoughts can lead to a greater degree of peace. The body and mind need to be in a relaxed state in order enter into a deep level of meditation. The practice of awareness throughout the day is very important because it allows us to control consciously our thoughts and actions. We begin to have the choice over our mind rather than reacting to it.

Please enjoy a wonderful meditation by Martin Faulks[14] that uses focus on the breath to aid a calm awareness, so the mind can become free from thoughts.

In Conclusion

For us to really progress we need to invest time in conscious thoughts and actions using our will power at every given opportunity. To listen to our subconscious mind and help it resolve and reprogram the negative responses. Most importantly, learn to take time out and relax and develop our concentration skills in daily life. This way we are staying aware and focused throughout the day. Then we can truly shine like the red lion.

---

14 https://www.youtube.com/watch?v=KSzsnDW5QQU

PART III: ESTABLISHING MAGICAL EQUILIBRIUM

9. Why You Should Work with The Four Elements – Ray del Sole

The human beings in general and also spiritual students experience themselves as limited to their individual character with specific qualities, powers and abilities. 'I am this, I can only do that, but I cannot behave like xy as I have not his characteristics, talents, energy,' and so on. So we have naturally the different main characters according to the four elements with a dominance of one or two and a deficiency in the other elements. It is a natural state of imbalance with strengths and weaknesses. For example, someone might be well developed in the fire element with great will-power and good imagination but lacking emotional understanding, empathy. Someone else might be a brilliant thinker but lacking earth, not grounded. And so on. Now certainly people do their best to survive life with their specific imbalances, powers and deficiencies.

From the spiritual point of view, it is most important not only to survive with your personal powers but to unfold all elements in a well-balanced way in quality and quantity. This means perfection, perfect vitality, perfect diversity of powers, skills and virtues.

And now it is important to understand that ONLY this balance of the four elements is the key to total success and total happiness in life.

So you can try to get along in life with your individual talents, but at some point you will fail as you lack the energies which are needed. You cannot balance or answer everything in life with will power or with emotional reactions, with patience, intelligence and so on. Indeed, you should give the right, analogue answer to the question life puts to you. If a situation needs empathy, you cannot answer with the intellect. If you need to take action, you cannot answer with patience. And so on. And this is what you must understand. Instead of focusing on your individual powers to survive, you should focus on accomplishing the magical equilibrium to have the fitting answer for all questions which occur.

And here the only key is to undergo as soon as possible the breathing exercises which Bardon describes for the four elements. Only in this way you will be able to balance and nourish yourself.

EQUIPOISE: INSIGHTS INTO FOUNDATIONAL ASTRAL TRAINING

The four elements are the most important key for your liberation, for health, happiness, vitality, success and abundance. When you are balanced in this way, the dark forces, also fate, has no chance. You are untouchable. You are free to follow your higher sense in life, your mission!

PART III: ESTABLISHING MAGICAL EQUILIBRIUM

10. Training with The Four Elements – Ray del Sole

Bardon describes breathing, accumulating and projecting exercises for the work with the four elements. The whole training has a focus on the astral plane, the astral body.

I would like to add a few points which you can integrate into your training.

The four elements rule not only the astral realms but also the mental and the physical realms. On the mental plane we have fire with will-power, motivation, imagination and concentration. We have the air element with all functions of the intellect and of inspiration, third eye and so on. We have the water element with feeling alive, with the ability to perceive things, also with introspection, consideration and meditation, together with air. And we have the earth element with mental strength, endurance, authority, vital work of all mental aspects, a strong mind.

Bardon develops these aspects by specific mental exercises, but you can also influence your mind and mental body directly by the use of the elements. Simply do the breathing exercises with the idea that you are on the mental plane in your mental body, inhaling/accumulating the element energy. Now meditate that the element energy in your mental body activates, strengthens and refines all corresponding mental powers, skills and qualities. After a while you release the extra energies to come back to a normal level of energy. Certainly do this with all four elements.

Then I also suggest working with the four elements on the Akasha plane. Here you imagine yourself in the center – Akasha point – of your microcosm which you imagine 'as vast as the universe', as a vast space where you cannot perceive the borders. And now you imagine the element filling this vast space. You can add here the colors for fire = red, air = light-blue, water = green-blue, earth = brown. Now meditate that the element is penetrating your whole microcosm – body with aura – and simply filling you completely. This will have beneficial effects on you. So you can meditate about vitalizing, healing, activating effects. Or you can meditate now that you have the total power over the element. 'I am the master of the element. The element follows my will!' Something like this. Do it with all four elements. After a while release the extra energies.

For the physical plane I suggest taking a glass of water and charging it with the element. Program the water element to activate and strengthen the denser and densest aspects of the element energy in your body so that you gain total control and power over the element even on the level of the material body/world. If you like, you can put a pinch of sea salt into the water.

Besides using water, you could also make experiments with simple food like a host or maybe a cookie. Here it is good too when it is slightly salty. Or you can use also the corresponding herbs as fluid condensers in the cookies.

If you use real food and bigger amounts of food then it can cause problems with digestion – already when it is only charged with vital energy.

In conclusion, these are some extra techniques which you can use to improve your work with the elements.

PART III: ESTABLISHING MAGICAL EQUILIBRIUM

11. A Qabbalistic Approach for the Magical Equilibrium – Ray del Sole

The qabbalistic training is very comprehensive and offers possibilities which can keep you busy for many years. We can differentiate here between the preparation training, the training with formulas and later the training with complex formulas – the names of divine beings, the spirits of the spheres. A special training form has its focus on the development of specific states of mind, specific powers, abilities and qualities. This gives a short overview.

One major milestone in the whole qabbalistic training is the achievement of total power over the four elements. This aim can be reached in different ways.

I want to present here one way which also comes along with a higher form of magical equilibrium and the embodiment of highest 'god-forms'. Bardon points a little bit at this by giving short hints.

There are specific four-letter-formulas for total power over the four elements where each letter has a specific meaning for a specific plane of existence.

I want to describe here one way to do it but certainly there are also options for the master.

Basically, we approach this technique by the well-known idea that the body has four main regions corresponding to the four elements. Fire is head region, air is chest region, water is belly region and earth is legs region. Further on, we can say that the right arm/hand is electric fluid and the left arm/hand is magnetic fluid, which corresponds also perfectly with the air element in the chest.

This approach is normally taken for the realization of the magical equilibrium.

The first exercise is to charge the head with Sch, the chest with A, the belly with M and the legs with Ä. This lets you embody the highest and first letters in perfect equilibrium. So, you represent the highest god-form in total harmony. In the best case you realize the letters from the Akasha point of the single regions. And then you meditate about your divine state and total power over the four elements on all planes. You keep the letters in your body so that they are processed by your energy system.

Maybe one day later you do the second exercise. H in the head, C in the chest, N in the belly and I in the legs. You should perform each letter twice. Again, you do the meditation.

On the third day you do the third exercise. S in the head, L in the chest, W in the belly and F in the legs. You should perform each letter three times. Again, you do the meditation.

On the fourth day you do the last exercise. T in the head, H in the chest, G in the belly and R in the legs. You should perform each letter four times. Again, you do the meditation.

In conclusion you have done four exercises paying respect to all higher laws and for all three planes of existence plus the Akasha plane with the focus on being in high divine states, causing harmony in yourself and realizing total power over all four elements.

So this is a very healthy, powerful technique. Certainly, this technique requires a good preparation by the mystical training which Bardon describes.

PART III: ESTABLISHING MAGICAL EQUILIBRIUM

12. THE EMERALD TABLET – RONDA STARKEY

This is my commentary on the Emerald Tablet which is based on the work of Dennis Hauck, Carl Jung, alchemy, kundalini, my own experiences and insights and establishing magical equilibrium.

'True without falsehood certain, and most true.'

Here we are being asked to set aside everything we have ever been taught to believe including our personal perspectives, emotions, doctrines, prejudices, or anything that could possibly stand in our way or falsify the blueprint or ancient alchemical formula the Emerald Tablet contains. This is the alchemical recipe from a man/god, to a man/god on becoming a man/god. This is the recipe to obtain what many alchemists called the Spiritual Gold or The Great Work.

I feel it's also worth mentioning that the emerald gem stone is known as the revealer of truth. I felt this was worth referencing, as the Emerald Tablet is made out of a green emerald-type substance.

'That which is above is like that which is below, that which is below is like that which is above.'

This is related to the Law of Correspondence and the macro and micro. This universal law tells us our outer world is nothing more than a mirror or reflection of our inner world. Everything we think and say is reflected in our physical world and when these thoughts have feelings attached to them the reflection becomes even stronger.

This also reflects the idea of our universe being composed of multiple planes of existence – spiritual, physical, and mental. What we see happening in one of these planes will always be reflected in the others simultaneously. If we take a look at what we are manifesting in our physical world we are able to determine whether our inner world is balanced and in harmony.

Example: if we are angry, jealous, insecure, emotional, self-loathing in our inner thoughts and world then our outer world will reflect chaos. Nothing in our outer world can ever change without first making the changes and transforming what we hold inside of us.

This is when our soul mirror work and establishing an elemental equilibrium comes in and becomes a very important and valuable tool for our evolution. It's now important for us to take an authentic look into our soul. We must here begin to dig deep within our being to work on seeing and clearing old patterns and triggers not serving our higher purpose as well as taking inventory of all our positive and negative qualities we hold within ourselves. We must not only realize and accept these traits but now begin our work to transform our weak ones into something we can utilize constructively in our life. It's important we achieve this magical equilibrium in order to go much further and be successful. This is important preparatory work for the alchemist and the great work.

> The above-heavens, macro, and world soul.
> The below-earth, physical, micro and human soul.
> These all come together to make

'The miracle of one thing.'

'As all things were made from the meditation of one mind, so all things are born of one thing.'

The one thing being the first matter or primordial unifying force that we come from. This is also called Kether or can be represented as the point within the circle.

'Its father is the sun.'

This is talking about 'calcination' which is the first step in alchemy.

Psychologically this is speaking about destroying the ego and all our attachments to the material world. We destroy here whatever may stand in our way of genuine happiness. This can be a natural process we go through as we experience the highs and lows of life. We can also choose to do this deliberately through consistent and deep meditation practice as well as other intense spiritual exercises and practices. Whether natural or deliberate these

PART III: ESTABLISHING MAGICAL EQUILIBRIUM

practices will ignite the sacred fire within us that will lead to introspection, contemplation, and evaluation of our self. This a time we withdraw from the outer world to go deep within.

On a psychological level this will ignite the sacred fire within us that will help us burn off any excess we hold onto that's no longer needed. Our metabolic level is going to heat up. This is when our kundalini begins to wake and heat up in the base of our spine or root chakra. Many in this state will notice an increase in overall body temperature as well as heat in body parts especially the hands, feet, and spine. This is the sacred fire of purification that will burn and get rid of all standing in the way of its path.

'Its mother is the moon.'

This is related to the second step in alchemy which is known as 'dissolution'.

Psychologically this is when we begin to further break down artificial structures we hold in our psyche. We are releasing painful and traumatic memories, perceived faults, and parts of ourselves we felt were once rejected. The water in this stage is helping us being able to let go of what we no longer need. This is a time we must go deep within our subconscious to clear all we have been taught over the years. It's said that ninety five percent of our life is created by the subconscious mind. Its job is to store and retrieve data and works like a big memory bank. Once we learn how to clear this big memory bank we can then work on focusing and re-programming it with constructive, creative, and positive thoughts that will then begin to implement uplifting and productive patterns in our everyday life. If we implement this positive thinking in our daily life it will change not only our outlook on life but our entire blueprint of our creation.

We must let go here and allow all that we have deeply buried in our subconscious over many lifetimes to surface and be dealt with. When we have a repeated memory of one of our past lives, it usually means we have an attachment to it that it is surfacing so that it can be dealt with in this life in order to clear it and move forward in our evolution.

On a physical level all the chakras and channels in our body are opening and clearing. This is happening so our kundalini/magnetic/electric energies can travel upwards without blockages and obstacles in the way.

'The wind carries it in its belly.'

This is speaking of the third step in alchemy which is 'separation'.

On a psychological level we begin here to discover our true nature or essence. We begin to reclaim what the logical or rational part of our mind has always made us think is impossible. We begin here to think outside the box. We realize our own mind has been restricting and limiting us from understanding and expressing our full potential.

We get rid of things here such as beliefs we no longer need or that don't serve our higher purpose. We review the shadows, and the hidden dark, within us. We begin to own up and take responsibility for our past and future actions. We allow our dark thoughts and feelings to arise in order to identify repetitive and negative mental patterns and habits that we no longer need to hold onto. After this release and review we must decide what to discard and what to integrate into our new refined personality and energy. We are letting go of so much here so we can allow our true nature to shine through. At this point it becomes extremely important to us that our words match our actions. The ancients would call this preparation for rebirth. If we are not ready for this review in our physical life we will be forced to face and experience this review when we separate from our physical body at death. It's often referred to as the 'Life Review' in the astral realm. One way or another separation must happen before any type of rebirth can take place in any body or on any plane.

On a physical level separation is learning breath work and how to control it, and keep it flowing through the channels. Our breath work in unison with the energy of the spirit and soul will give us new energy, vitality and vibration.

This is happening at a solar plexus level. Our breath is now helping carry the energies and kundalini upwards.

'The earth is its nurse.'

This is the fourth step in alchemy which is 'conjunction'.

On a psychological level this is the union of our masculine and feminine into our personality and into an intuitive state of consciousness. This is considered the marriage of the sun and the moon, or ultimately the

PART III: ESTABLISHING MAGICAL EQUILIBRIUM

union of our soul and spirit. This is where we begin to merge our opposites or polars.

The ancient alchemist often would call this the lesser stone.

We now begin to notice more synchronized events in our life. We also begin to put the pieces together of the big puzzle we call life.

This is when we begin to be able to discern what needs to be done to achieve union of monad and to also be able to obtain lasting enlightenment.

On a physical level this is when we begin to use our sexual energies to accelerate our personal transformation and evolution. We raise these energies into our heart chakra. These energies are used to open, clear, and strengthen the heart chakra.

It's very important the heart chakra be open, as it is the bridge for our higher and lower chakras as well as our kundalini. If this is not open the kundalini will be forced to stay in the lower chakras and will not be able to rise further.

Once we open and clear the heart chakra we will notice our evolution begins to accelerate. This is also where we want to learn to raise our sexual energies at this stage in alchemy but I will leave it at that. Learning to utilize our sexual energies for our evolution is a book in itself.

'Separate the earth from the fire, the subtle from the gross, gently and with great ingenuity.'

This is the fifth step in alchemy known as 'fermentation'.

On a psychological level this is when we become super inspired by the heavens or spiritual forces from above. This is the stage where the alchemist becomes inspired, energized, and enlightened.

Out of the alchemist's blackness of putrefaction comes yellow ferment, which appears as the 'golden wax' flowing out of the foul manner of our souls.

This is the stage where we see the peacock's tail or its colors. Its brilliance is truly breathtaking. By seeing this we know we are being guided by a higher power and are on the right track.

Fermentation can be achieved through intense prayer, deep meditation, or even the intense desire for a spiritual union. A more practical way would be by breaking down our psyche and personality through deep introspection, reflection, and contemplation work.

On a physical level this is when our pineal and pituitary are open, purified, and begin to work in unison.

'It rises from earth to heaven and descends back again to earth.'

This is the sixth stage of alchemy known as 'distillation'.

On a psychological level this is the agitation and sublimation of psychic forces which is necessary to ensure we have rid ourselves of all impurities and rid ourselves of whatever we have left of the ego.

Here is when we begin to become free of our identity. We have become free of emotions and sentimentality. This is the stage where we purify the unborn self. We truly lose the only identity we have ever known.

On a physical level we are now raising our kundalini and energies from the lower chakras all the way up to the crown and the brain. We are also now raising our sexual energies up through the heart to the brain which is releasing a liquid light to help in the evolution of our mind. We are now storing our sexual energies in the brain to use towards spiritual transformation. The third eye, pituitary, and pineal are releasing this light or fluid on the brain. This begins to form our new solid body of light. We are now beginning our return to the primordial or the Garden of Eden, the place we once started from.

'Thus will obtain the glory of the whole universe, all obscurity will be clear to you. This is the greatest force of all powers because it overcomes every subtle thing and penetrates every solid thing.'

This is the final stage of alchemy known as 'coagulation'.

On a psychological level we are now living and experiencing an entire new way of being. We are now living beyond all people, places and things.

This is what many ancients would call the true rebirth.

We have at this point created a permanent vehicle for our consciousness to travel, which many sages would call the blue sphere.

PART III: ESTABLISHING MAGICAL EQUILIBRIUM

The blue sphere allows us to freely travel the upper and lower planes. We are no longer captivated by the mental, physical, and astral matrix, or illusions.

We now have an understanding of how our mental, astral, and physical bodies work separately as well as in unison.

On a physical level we are experiencing massive amounts of fluid on the brain which is being released through the light which the pineal and pituitary are producing.

This is the stage where we have finally returned to what can be called the Garden of Eden or point zero.

The energies of masculine – Adam – and feminine – Eve – have been purified, refined and are ready to merge in a divine union in the third eye. These energies then move as one up through the crown chakra, as the left and right hemispheres of the brain are now bridged together forming a glorious rainbow bridge or arc.

We can go through many of these stages more than once and they should not be only thought of in a linear context. Each time we repeat these stages we are refining our energy more and more. We continue to repeat these stages but through higher frequencies each time we do. In this stage we are integrating all previous six stages, but this is not the end of our transformation by any means as we are now in tune and able to act upon higher wisdom, for we now know that our thoughts, feelings, and actions can affect the entire universe by working like a domino effect.

Coagulation is the final stage in alchemy or the end which we now realize was only the beginning, or the return and merge back with the primordial. This is the return to the source. This is what ancient alchemists considered obtaining the 'gold' or 'great work'.

'From this grew wonderful adaptations which thus is the way, therefore I am called Hermes Trismegistus having the three parts of philosophy of the whole world.'

I feel he is speaking of mental, physical, and spiritual as well as the trinity which is a big key to how the universe operates.

EQUIPOISE: INSIGHTS INTO FOUNDATIONAL ASTRAL TRAINING

All things in the universe consist of the trinity. I feel this is what Hermes is trying to convey. He is showing us that he as well as all of us are a part of the trinity of the entire universe and existence.

PART III: ESTABLISHING MAGICAL EQUILIBRIUM

13. How Greed Obstructs Efficient Self-Transformation – Virgil

I have to admit that I used to be a greedy person. Many people think of greed as the desire for more money. In that sense, I wasn't greedy. While I've always had respect for money and its value, I was never obsessed with getting more of it than I really needed. That said, I was still greedy. In Zen Buddhism, greed is seen as the unconditional desire for more, and this is also the way I have come to see greed. Whether a specific instance of greed involves a desire to acquire more money, a desire to read more books, or a desire to have more friends doesn't matter. The belief that more is always better is the root of greed, regardless of whether it is money, books, or friends we are speaking of.

During the summer of 2008, I had the goal of reading two books a week. That's a lot of books to read in one summer. I succeeded because my greed was strong. In other words, I felt strongly that reading more books was better. Later, as I reflected on that summer, I realized that I didn't really get anything out of it. What matters isn't the amount you read, as a greedy person like myself believed, but the quality and thoroughness of your reading. Did you try to consume as many books as possible the way a dragon tries to hoard as much gold as possible, or did you really study each book carefully, taking your time to reflect upon the major lessons within it and to extract the key insights?

Consider two Bardonists - Bardonist A and Bardonist B. Bardonist A is greedy. He thinks the more commentaries he has, the better. He spends a lot of effort collecting commentaries. Bardonist B isn't greedy. He doesn't spend a lot of effort collecting commentaries because he doesn't believe that the more commentaries he has, the better. Instead, he is grateful for what he already has, which is just IIH. Because he is grateful for having IIH, he appreciates the book. He seeks to get as much as he can from this one book he has, because he understands its true value. Bardonist B is likely to end up with a much more solid understanding of IIH than Bardonist A has, despite the fact that Bardonist A has ten commentaries and Bardonist B has none. More commentaries isn't necessarily better. More of anything isn't necessarily better. Yet, how many people have fully realized this? How many people are truly devoid of greed?

In the Bardon community, I see a lot of greedy Bardonists. I see people trying to buy more books about the Bardon system because they think more is always better. I see people spending more time practicing the exercises of IIH because they think more is always better. Even as an author, I've had to struggle with greed. When I first started writing, I figured that the more readers I had, the better. Now I realize that it's not about finding more readers. It's about finding the right readers. Similarly, it's not about reading more books about the Bardon system. It's about reading the right books in the right way. It's not about spending more time practicing the exercises of IIH. It's about spending the right amount of time, in other words enough time to make steady progress but not so much time that you are overtraining and injuring yourself while neglecting other important aspects of your life, like your loved ones.

So, what does this have to do with the astral work of Step 2? Well, I often see students at this step trying to collect as many self-transformation techniques as they can find. They think that the more self-transformation techniques they know, the more likely they are to succeed in ridding themselves of their negative traits and developing the positive traits they need in order to establish magical equilibrium. This frantic effort to collect as many self-transformation techniques as possible is an example of greed. Knowing more self-transformation techniques isn't necessarily better. It doesn't guarantee that your chances of succeeding in the Step 2 astral work will increase.

Gratitude is a powerful weapon against greed. Be grateful for what you have. Bardon provides you with some fantastic self-transformation techniques in IIH, including conscious eating, conscious breathing, and use of the magic of water. Being grateful for them will motivate you to get the most out of them. To better understand what I mean, consider the conscious eating technique.

Conscious eating is the single most powerful self-transformation technique accessible to Step 2 Bardonists that I have ever come across. That said, how many Bardonists are tapping into the full power of this technique? A significant number of Bardonists impregnate their food and then eat it absent-mindedly or while watching television. This is making a half-assed

PART III: ESTABLISHING MAGICAL EQUILIBRIUM

effort to use the technique. As a friend of mine likes to say, 'Never half-ass anything. Always use your whole ass.' Think about the Bardonists who impregnate their food with a positive trait and then eat that food while believing with full conviction that the food is the trait. When they impregnate spaghetti with patience and then swallow it, they know with every ounce of their being that it is not spaghetti they are swallowing but patience. The people who practice conscious eating in this manner will see results much sooner than the people who simply impregnate their food and eat it mindlessly. That isn't really conscious eating, but mindless eating of food that happens to be impregnated.

So if you're asking yourself: 'Where can I learn more self-transformation techniques to use?' you may be asking yourself the wrong question. Furthermore, you may want to add a greed-related trait to your black soul mirror. A better question to ask yourself would be 'How can I get the most out of the self-transformation techniques I already know?' Improving your mastery over the self-transformation techniques you already know may be a wiser use of your time than reading more books and articles to learn more self-transformation techniques.

And that's really the key to it – wisdom. My intent in writing this article isn't to discourage you from trying to learn insightful information that can help you transform yourself into a more pure and balanced person. However, when you do read books in search of more self-transformation techniques, make sure that this is an endeavor that stems from wisdom rather than one that is driven by greed. I'm not saying that more is never better, because sometimes it is. All I'm saying is that more isn't always better. While greed is the erroneous belief that more is always better, the opposite of greed isn't the conviction that more is never better. It's the wisdom that lets you know when more is better and when it isn't.

14. Conscious Eating and the Tetragrammaton – Virgil

If most people looked at the Tetragrammaton, they would probably think of it as having four parts, with each letter being one of the parts. This is a valid and traditional way of viewing the Tetragrammaton, but it's not the only one. Many Kabbalists think of the upper tip of the Yod as being its own thing, distinct from the rest of the Yod. With this in mind, the Tetragrammaton can be thought of as having five parts – the tip of the Yod, the rest of the Yod, the first Heh, the Vav, and the final Heh.

In his book *Body Mind, and Soul* Rabbi Yitzchak Ginzburgh explains how the process of using spiritual techniques to heal others can be divided into five phases that correspond to the five parts of the Tetragrammaton. The process of healing that he describes is very similar to the process of conscious eating. By seeing analogies between the process of conscious eating – like healing oneself of imbalances – and the process of healing others, the process of conscious eating can also be divided into five phases that correspond to the five parts of the Tetragrammaton:

>Tip of the Yod: Becoming conscious
>Rest of the Yod: Becoming focused
>First Heh: Generating the idea of the positive trait in one's mind
>Vav: Projecting the idea of the positive trait into the akasha of the food
>Final Heh: Eating the food and assimilating the trait into oneself

Some additional food for thought can also be generated by reflecting on the correspondences between the five parts of the Tetragrammaton and the sephiroth of the Tree of Life. If you are a practitioner of Rawn's TMO form of magic, then you are already familiar with the following set of correspondences:

>Tip of the Yod: Kether
>Rest of the Yod: Chockmah

PART III: ESTABLISHING MAGICAL EQUILIBRIUM

First Heh: Binah
Vav: Tiphereth
Final Heh: Malkuth

The tip of the Yod corresponds to the sephirah Kether. Kether is consciousness in its most pure and undifferentiated form. It is the gate through which consciousness first flows into the vacancy generated by *tzimtzum* to create the universe. This is why the tip of the Yod corresponds to the process of becoming conscious. Conscious eating is magic. You can't do magic if you aren't conscious or mindful. Before you've mastered the Step 1 present-mindedness/mindfulness exercise, you'll probably spend a lot of your time in a mindless/absent-minded state. However, you can't impregnate food in this state. In order to impregnate food, you must first leave your state of mindlessness/absent-mindedness and be conscious/mindful/aware.

The rest of the Yod corresponds to Chockmah. This is the sephirah that corresponds to pure force. The focused mind is a force in its own right. It is the force that ultimately transforms the food into the positive trait.

The first Heh corresponds to Binah. Binah is a divine womb. Just as a baby is formed in a womb, so the idea of the positive trait is formed in the mind during the third phase of conscious eating.

Vav corresponds to the sephirah Tiphereth. This sephirah is associated with positive transformation. Needless to say, when you project the idea of the positive trait into the akasha of the food, the food is transformed. In Western esotericism, the vice associated with Tiphereth is self-importance – referred to by some as pride. When you realize that you have the power to transform food using your mind, you may feel a sense of self-importance. That sense of self-importance will likely be a serious detriment to your magical advancment. As students of magic, we strive to become servants of Divine Providence. The ability to transform food by impregnating it is given to us so that we may become more effective servants of Divine Providence, and not because we are somehow more important than those who don't know how to impregnate food.

Tiphereth is traditionally seen as the child of Chockmah and Binah. The process of projecting the idea of the positive trait into the akasha of the food is only possible because we have the idea, via the third phase, and the force to project it with, via the second phase. Thus, just as Tiphereth is created from Chockmah and Binah, so the fourth phase of conscious eating is founded upon the second and third phases.

On the Tree of Life, Tiphereth is located at the center, so it is the sephirah through which the flow of divine consciousness is transmitted from the top half of the Tree of Life to the bottom half. Similarly, it is through the fourth phase of conscious eating that the idea of the positive trait is transmitted from your mind to the akasha of the food.

The final Heh corresponds to the sephirah Malkuth. Malkuth is a purely receptive sephirah. The other sephiroth receive light from the sephiroth above and transmit light to the sephiroth below. There are no sephiroth below Malkuth, so it only receives light. The last step of conscious eating, which is to eat the food and assimilate the positive trait into yourself, is a receptive activity. You are receiving the food into yourself, and you are receiving the trait into your personality. Do not equate receptivity with passivity. In other words, do not assume that just because an action is receptive in nature one must do it passively. Listening is a receptive process, however I'm sure you've heard the term 'active listening'. Michael Nichols, the author of *The Lost Art of Listening*, doesn't like the phrase 'active listening' because genuine listening is an inherently active process. Therefore, it is redundant to include the word 'active' in front of the word 'listening' to describe it. Similarly, the process of receiving the food into yourself needs to be done actively. You are free to interpret for yourself what this means. For me, it means paying attention, being aware, and believing with full conviction that the morsel of food you are swallowing is the positive trait you are trying to develop. Mindless eating is not active.

www.ingramcontent.com/pod-product-compliance
Lightning Source LLC
LaVergne TN
LVHW051054080426
835508LV00019B/1875